DUTCH INTERIOR

DUTCH INTERIOR

Postwar Poetry of the
Netherlands and Flanders

Edited by JAMES S HOLMES
and WILLIAM JAY SMITH

With an Introduction by CEES BUDDINGH'

Columbia University Press
NEW YORK   1984

Preparation and publication of this work were supported by
the Translation and Publication Programs of the Foundation for
the Promotion of the Translation of Dutch Literary Works, and
the Prince Bernhard Fund, to which acknowledgment is grate-
fully made.

Grateful acknowledgment is also made for the assistance pro-
vided by the Translation Center of Columbia University and
the Pushkin Fund.

Library of Congress Cataloging in Publication Data
Main entry under title:

Dutch interior.

  Bibliography: p.
  Includes index.
    1. Dutch poetry—20th century—Translations into
English.   2. Flemish poetry—20th century—Translations
into English.   3. English poetry—Translations from
Dutch.   I. Holmes, James S, 1924–   II. Smith, William Jay,
1918–
PT5475.E5D87 1984   839.3′1164′08   83-27322
ISBN 0-231-05746-6

Columbia University Press
New York   Guildford, Surrey
Copyright © 1984 Columbia University Press
All rights reserved
Printed in the United States of America

Clothbound editions of Columbia University Press books are
Smyth-sewn and printed on permanent and durable acid-free paper.

Book design by Ken Venezio

Contents

THE FIFTIES: THE EXPERIMENTAL REVOLT   33

Preface

To study the history of the world's art without considering Dutch painting—from Rembrandt and Vermeer (and the Jan Steen of the Dutch interior) to Van Gogh, Mondrian, and Karel Appel—would be madness. How strange, then, that so little is known of what the Dutch have achieved in most other art forms. In the case of poetry, at least, it is an unwarranted ignorance. It is to be hoped that this anthology, the first full-scale presentation of contemporary poetry in Dutch to be issued in English, will help to ameliorate the situation.

First, a remark about the word "Dutch." Most frequently the term is an indicator of nationality: of or having to do with the Netherlands or, its often-applied but inaccurate synonym, Holland. It is in this sense that the word is used in such expressions as "the Dutch," "Dutch painting," or (in its usual meaning) "Dutch interior." But "Dutch" is as well an indicator of a language, one which is the native tongue not only of most of the inhabitants of the Netherlands but also of the entire northern half of Belgium . . . where, to compound the confusion, it is often called Flemish. Add a number of people in the Netherlands Antilles and Surinam and a scattered handful in Indonesia, Zaire, Australia, Canada, and the United States, and you arrive at a total of something over twenty million speakers. Obviously, then, when the word "Dutch" is used in connection with the products of language there is often some confusion. This anthology presents the major poets of the postwar period from the entire Dutch-speaking corner of Europe, both the Netherlands in the north and Flanders in the south.

Such an anthology should of course be strictly objective in the selection of both poets and poems. But objectivity, if devoutly to be wished, is a thing unattainable in the arts. Still, subjectivities can at least to some degree be balanced against one another. During the course of this long-planned project we sought advice from a number of poets and critics in the Low Countries, among whom special mention should be made of Gerrit Borgers, Gerrit Kouwenaar, Eddy van Vliet, and above all Cees Buddingh'. The end result of this consultation was a list of forty-five poets whose work can, we hope, be considered representative of the best that has been written in the Netherlands and Flanders since World War II. On the basis of this list, the first editor brought together all that he could find or solicit of existing and new translations into English, adding to them a large number of new renderings of his own. After a preliminary selection in which he pared the pile of texts down to a massive array three times as long as what is represented here, the two editors together mulled long and closely over that array to reduce it to a manageable size. Grateful though we are, then, for the aid and advice of others, praise or blame for the final selection must fall on our shoulders alone. With two qualifications: for some fine poems there are simply no fine translations, and for some fine poets there are fewer translations than for others.

During the exciting but sometimes tedious task of putting the anthology together, we have received unstinting help and support from the Foundation for the Translation of Dutch Literary Works in Amsterdam, and in particular from Scott Rollins of its staff. To it and to him we are deeply grateful, as we are also to the Translation Center at Columbia University, which has lent its encouragement to the project over a period of years. Thanks are moreover due to the many translators represented here, who responded to an appeal by supplying us with extensive files of their translations, and among them specifically to Wanda Boeke, who drafted a translation of the introduction on which the present version is based. Acknowledgment is further due the University of Iowa International Writing Program and its former director Paul Engle for having urged the first editor to work on the project during his stay in Iowa City as a Fellow of the Program in 1975, and to the

Rob Amsterdam Gallery in New York and its director Dai Evans, who encouraged him to devote a good part of his time to the anthology during his stay at the gallery in Spring 1982 as Poet in Residence. And finally we owe great gratitude to Sonja Smith and Hans van Marle, who have put up with us over the months as we have alternately grumbled and rejoiced in our editorial labors.

JAMES S HOLMES
WILLIAM JAY SMITH

Acknowledgments

The editors of *Dutch Interior* and the Columbia University Press wish to thank the poets, translators, editors of reviews, and publishers for allowing them to reprint the following material. Every effort has been made to trace the original sources of the English texts included. Possible errors or omissions will be corrected in subsequent printings, provided notification is given of their existence. The Dutch texts that are the sources of the translations are listed in the section "Bibliography and Sources."

Botteghe Oscure (Rome) for Hans Lodeizen's "La voix du peuple" from no. 15 (Summer 1955) and Hans Andreus' "Countryside in France" from no. 18 (Autumn 1956)

Remco Campert, *In the Year of the Strike* (London: Rapp & Whiting, 1968) for Campert's "Poetry Is an Act," "Sparrows," "This Happened Everywhere," "Would You Believe It," "Eric Dolphy," and "City Park"

Carcanet (Oxford, England) for Hans Andreus' "Horror Story" from the Dutch Poetry Supplement (June 1963)

Chapman (Hamilton, Scotland) for Gerrit Kouwenaar's "Found Subjects" from vol. 2, no. 5/6 (1974)

City Lights Books Inc. for "Uncle Carl: A Home Movie" by J. Bernlef and "The Indigo Eater" by Lucebert, which appeared in *Nine Dutch Poets,* Lawrence Ferlinghetti and Scott Rollins, eds., copyright © 1982, City Lights Books

Contemporary Literature in Translation (Vancouver) for J. Bernlef's "Erik Satie," Jacques Hamelink's "For the Shadow" and "The Ammonite," and Eddy van Vliet's "Stockholm" from no. 32 (1981)

Delta: A Review of Arts Life and Thought in the Netherlands and the Delta International Publication Foundation (both Amsterdam) for Gerrit Achterberg's "Skin," "Bridegroom," "Ichthyology," and "Ballad of the Store Clerk" (from the issue for Summer 1958); Cees Buddingh's "Sufficient unto the Day" (Autumn 1967); Remco Campert's "Letters" (Spring/Summer 1968); Hugo Claus' "Family," "Marsyas," and "The Mother" (Autumn 1958); Jan G. Elburg's "Young Old Young Old," "The Axes Rust," and "Knowledge of What Is" (Spring 1964); Gust Gils' "How Fine N'est-ce pas" (Autumn 1960) and "Fairy Tale" (Autumn 1966); Mark Insingel's "With Heads Held High" (Spring 1973); Rutger Kopland's "Among the Flowers" (Winter 1972); Gerrit Kouwenaar's "Without Names," "Without Colors," and "Like an Object" (Spring 1968); Hans Lodeizen's "He Was the Best of All" and "The World an Old Music Box" (Winter 1958–59); Lucebert's "I Try in Poetic Fashion" (Autumn 1960) and "The Great Wall" (Autumn 1968); Hanny Michaelis' "We Carry Eggshells," "Irredeemably Buried," and "Somewhere in the House" (Summer 1973); Adriaan Morriën's "The Use of a Wall Mirror" (Summer 1970); Hugues C. Pernath's "Since Dew the Day," "The Answer Is" (both Summer 1964), "He Represented a Skin" (Summer 1963), and "Unchastity" (Spring 1971); Sybren Polet's "Celebration" (Summer 1962); Paul Rodenko's "He" (Autumn 1962); Paul Snoek's "Rustic Landscape" (Summer 1966); Hans Verhagen's "Hans Verhagen & Son" (Autumn 1965); Eddy van Vliet's "Birth" (Autumn 1973); and Leo Vroman's "Indian Summer" (Hudson Number 1958)

Dimension (The University of Texas, Austin, Texas) for H. C. ten Berge's "The Hartlaub Gull," Judith Herzberg's "Tree Surgeon," three parts of Hans Faverey's "Chrysanthemums,

Rowers," and Jacques Hamelink's "Stonetalk" from the Special Dutch Issue (1978)

Gust Gils, *Levend voorwerp* (Animate Object) (Amsterdam: Bezige Bij, 1969) for Gils' "Two Japanese Poems"

Helix (Ivanhoe, Australia) for Hugo Claus' "In Flanders Fields" from no. 7/8 (1981)

Konrad Hopkins and Ronald van Roekel, eds., *Quartet: An Anthology of Dutch and Flemish Poetry* (Paisley, Scotland: Wilfion Books, 1978) for Judith Herzberg's "Burying" and "Sneakers" and Eddy van Vliet's "In These Exhausting Lowlands"

Mark Insingel, *Posters* (Bruges: Orion/The Hague: Scheltens & Giltay, 1974) for Insingel's "Descartes"

International Poetry Review (Princeton, New Jersey) for Lucebert's"Breyten Breytenbach May Look at the Moon" from vol. 7, no. 1 (Spring 1981)

Pierre Kemp, *An English Alphabet* (Amsterdam: Spectatorpers, 1961) for all poems by Kemp

Gerrit Komrij, *The Comreigh Critter* (Amsterdam & New York: C. J. Aarts, 1982) for all poems by Komrij

Rutger Kopland, *An Empty Place to Stay* (San Francisco: Twin Peaks Press, 1977) for Kopland's "Johnson Brothers Ltd.," "Old Country House," "Young Lettuce," "Blackbird," "No Generation," and "Tarzan Once More"

Literary Review (Fairleigh Dickinson University, Madison, New Jersey) for Gerrit Achterberg's "House" from vol. 5, no. 2 (Winter 1961–62)

The London Magazine (London) for Remco Campert's "A President in His Country Residence" from the issue for March 1961, and Hans Lodeizen's "Evening at the Merrills" from that for February 1960

Lucebert Edited by Lucebert (London: Marlborough Fine Art, 1963) for Lucebert's "School of Poetry"

Lucebert, *The Tired Lovers They Are Machines* (London: Transgravity Press, 1974) for the title poem

Modern Poetry in Translation (London) for Hans Andreus' "Words for You"; Cees Buddingh's "Historical Materialism," "Petit salon des indépendants," and "The Monkey"; Patrick Conrad's "Roxy's," "The Illegal Operation," and "The Back Seat Dodge '38"; Judith Herzberg's "Kitten," "Magic," "After a Photo," and "A Child's Mirror"; Adriaan Morriën's "Gastronomy"; Sybren Polet's "Shadow" and "Alienation & Alliteration"; K. Schippers' "Jigsaw Puzzle" and "Grains of Sand on a Radio"; and Riekus Waskowsky's "Salt Peanuts" and "If by Eternity" (all from no. 27/28, Summer 1976)

Adriaan Morriën, *The Use of a Wall Mirror* (San Francisco: Twowindows Press, 1970) for Morriën's "Shipwreck" and "My Parents' House"

New Directions Publishing Corporation (New York) for Sybren Polet's "Re-education" from *Living Space: Poems of the Dutch "Fiftiers,"* New Directions, 1979, copyright © 1979 by the Foundation for the Promotion of the Translation of Dutch Literary Works. Reprinted by permission.

Peter Nijmeijer, ed., *Four Dutch Poets* (London: Transgravity Press, 1976) for Lucebert's "9000 Jackals Swimming to Boston," Gerrit Kouwenaar's "Place: Somewhere" and "4 Variations On," and Sybren Polet's "The Human Use of Human Beings"

W. W. Norton & Company, Inc. (New York) for "Statue" and "Accountability" by Gerrit Achterberg, translated from the Dutch by Adrienne Rich, reprinted from *Necessities of Life: Poems 1962–1965* by Adrienne Rich, copyright © 1966 by W. W. Norton & Company, Inc. Reprinted by permission.

Odyssey Review (Richmond, Virginia) for Gerrit Achterberg's "Word," "Ravel's Bolero," "Lullaby," and "Sleepwalking" from the issue for December 1961

Poet (Madras, India) for J. Bernlef's "The Sound of Matter," Cees Buddingh's "The Music Makers," and Riekus Waskowsky's "That the Sun Will Rise Tomorrow" from the Dutch Number (September 1970)

Poetry Australia (Five Dock, N.S.W.) for Gerrit Kouwenaar's "Elba" and Hans Lodeizen's "Jim I Would Like to Know" from no. 52 (1974)

Poetry International and the Rotterdam Arts Foundation (both Rotterdam) for Cees Buddingh's "Ode to the Yorkshire Dales," Fritzi Harmsen van Beek's "Good Morning? Heavenly Madam Ping," and Gerrit Kouwenaar's "Landscape Left Behind" from Poetry International handout sheets

Prospice (Breakish, Skye, Scotland) for Hugo Claus' "Ambush" and Gerrit Kouwenaar's "Hand, Etc." from no. 5 (1976)

Scott Rollins, ed., *Ten Lowlands Poets* (Amsterdam: Dremples, 1979) for H. H. ter Balkt's "The Mill," Jacques Hamelink's "The Pyrenees: 1, 6," K. Schippers' "How a Guitar Can Lie on a Chair," Jotie T'Hooft's "Lenny Bruce Fixes" and "Starships," and Ad Zuiderent's "Appealing to the Imagination"

Shantih (Brooklyn, New York) for Lucebert's "Slowly I Begin to Play the Game" from vol. 2, no. 4 (Spring/Summer 1973)

Paul Snoek and Willem M. Roggeman, eds., *1945–1970: A Quarter Century of Poetry from Belgium* (Brussels & The Hague: Manteau, 1970) for Patrick Conrad's "Zeppelins," Mark Insingel's "The Gardens, Betrayed," and Hugues C. Pernath's "Index: 31–34"

The Times Literary Supplement (London) for Hans Andreus' "Mulish" from the issue for October 13, 1961, and Rutger Kopland's "Conversation" from that for August 7, 1981

Twayne Publishers (Boston) for all the poems by Bert Schierbeek from *Shapes of the Voice* by Bert Schierbeek, published Twayne, 1977

Hans Verhagen, *Stars over Bombay* (London: Transgravity Press, 1971) for Verhagen's "Cancer" and "Stars"

Leo Vroman, *262 Gedichten* (262 Poems) (Amsterdam: Querido, 1974) for Vroman's "Feathers," "The Horse of Death," and "Daily Preparations"

Hans van de Waarsenburg, ed., *Five Contemporary Dutch Poets* (Merrick, New York: Cross-Cultural Communications, 1979) for J. Bernlef's "The Art of Being Second"

Hans van de Waarsenburg, ed., *Five Contemporary Flemish Poets* (Merrick, New York: Cross-Cultural Communications, 1979) for Herman de Coninck's "Frédérique, or How I Became a Historian" and "Every Day Here Is Like This"

Manfred Wolf, ed., *Change of Scene* (San Francisco: Twowindows Press, 1969) for Gust Gils' "Ballad of a Perennially Misunderstood Man"

Manfred Wolf, ed., *The Shape of Houses* (Berkeley, California: Twowindows Press, 1974) for Judith Herzberg's "Vocation" and "Yiddish" and Hanny Michaelis' "Involuntarily, Almost," "Three Flights Up," and "The Body"

Writing in Holland and Flanders and the Foundation for the Promotion of the Translation of Dutch Literary Works (Amsterdam) for H. H. ter Balkt's "The Animals' Crusade" and "Elegy of the Hogs" (from no. 38, Spring 1981); Remco Campert's "Imagine" and "Hurrah, Hurrah" (no. 35, Summer 1978); Herman de Coninck's "The Rhinoceros" and "A Briton" (no. 38); Hans Faverey's "Staring at an Empty Space," "First the Message Kills," and two parts of "Chrysanthemums, Rowers" (no. 38); Judith Herzberg's "The Dishwasher" (no. 36, Spring 1979); Roland Jooris' "Minimal," "Village," "Density," "Cuckoo," and "Writing" (no. 38); Rutger Kopland's "With Green Patches" (no. 32, Summer 1973); Hans Tentije's "Icarian Is the Sea" and "Barges, Rivers" (no. 38); Eddy van Vliet's "The Shoreline Doesn't Change" and "Old Champagne Glass" (no. 38); and Leo Vroman's "To Whom This May Concern" and "February" (no. 32)

Ad Zuiderent, *Cycling, Recycling* (Amsterdam: Arbeiderspers and One World Poetry, 1984) for Zuiderent's "Return to Solitude," "House on the River," and "Gesture of Understanding"

Introduction

In February 1950 I happened upon Selden Rodman's *Anthology of Modern Poetry*. I had been writing verse myself since 1935 and was tremendously interested in "modern poetry." I knew the work of the French Surrealists, the German Dadaists such as Hans Arp and Kurt Schwitters, Auden, Spender, Mac-Niece, and Dylan Thomas among the English and Eliot, Stevens, and Pound among the Americans, and then, of course, García Lorca. I thought it was all wonderful. I made some translations of Péret and Éluard, and some of Auden and Lorca. A friend of mine translated *The Wasteland*. But our translations were of little use: the editors of the Dutch literary reviews were not impressed; this stuff was unheard of, crazy.

For more than ten years I had been cut off from foreign poetry, first by the five-year German occupation and then by a second bout with tuberculosis shortly after the war was over. I had spent the last two and a half years in a sanatorium bed, and Rodman's anthology was my first renewed encounter with what I felt were the sources of modern poetry. I devoured his introduction, particularly the list of what he considered the distinctive characteristics of modernity.

Unfortunately I had to admit that, with a few rare but notable exceptions, no poetry fitting Rodman's description was being written in the Netherlands. There was no truly modern poetry in Dutch. And it did not seem likely that the situation would change very quickly.

But a few months later I came across a copy of the little magazine *Blurb,* published and edited by Simon Vinkenoog, a young Dutchman who worked for UNESCO in Paris. Soon after that I found some copies of Remco Campert and Rudy Kousbroek's magazine *Braak* (Fallow). What was printed in these two mimeographed reviews was completely different from the fare of the established Dutch monthlies and quarterlies. The next year, 1951, saw the publication of Vinkenoog's *Atonaal* (Atonal), an anthology of poetry by a group of new writers in Dutch, the "Experimentalists," as they were most often referred to later. The same year also marked the publication of Lucebert's first book of poems, *Triangel in de jungel* (Triangle in the Jungle), and of Bert Schierbeek's experimental "novel" *Het boek ik* (The Book I). . . . And then there was no longer any doubt about it: suddenly a whole new generation of poets had come into its own, including, among others, Hans Andreus, Jan G. Elburg, Gerrit Kouwenaar, Jan Hanlo, Paul Rodenko, Hans Lodeizen (who had died very young in 1950), and the Fleming Hugo Claus. In poetry wonders had not ceased.

In 1954 I published a long essay about the new, still highly controversial writing that was coming to the fore. In it I presented a list, more or less along Rodman's lines, setting out six distinctive features that bound the writers of the fifties together as a "school" and showed how their poetry deviated sharply from the kind of poetry previously in vogue:

1. They resist the dictates of anachronistic prosodic forms, such as the sonnet and the iambic line.
2. They avail themselves to a greater or lesser degree of an increased freedom in imagery that stems from the discovery of automatic writing.
3. The poetic connections in their poems are predominantly associative rather than causal, as in previous poetry.
4. The anecdotal poem that played such an important part in the work of the Criterium group* has completely disappeared from the picture.

---

*A group of poets gathered around *Criterium* (Criterion), an influential review in the immediate postwar period. One of the poets closely associated with it was Adriaan Morriën.

5. Instead of emotional unity there is frequently emotional multiplicity.
6. Their poems are not primarily directed at the reader's consciousness, particularly not those poems that have an expressly experimental character and so might be called "stones in the pools of consciousness," which achieve an ever deeper effect the further the ripples they cause spread outward.

And I concluded with the words: "If there were no Experimentalists, they would have to be invented, or, at any rate, their poetry would have to be."

At the outset there was fierce resistance to the work of the Experimental group on the part of the traditional poetry critics and readers (one Dadaist poem by Jan Hanlo even led to questions in Parliament). But the resistance diminished with the passage of time. Within a few years, the Experimentalists, joined in the meantime by Sybren Polet, were not only pretty well accepted, but the group was in fact considered by many to be the very touchstone of what poetry should be. "I came, I saw, I conquered," Lucebert might easily have said on the memorable occasion when he was crowned "Emperor of the Generation of the Fifties" in one of the group's more turbulent manifestations. His objective, "to give expression to/ the expanse of life at its fullest," became the objective of every up-and-coming poet. Like the cult of the sonnet that had gone before, there now quickly emerged an equally depressing cult of imitative experimentalism.

In those same years it was becoming increasingly clear that, although the writers of the fifties had presented themselves as a group and, whenever necessary (and at the outset it was very often necessary), had formed a common front, the differences among them were at least as marked as their similarities. Lucebert was influenced chiefly by Hans Arp and Friedrich Hölderlin, Remco Campert by American poets, Sybren Polet by modern technology and Whitman. After a brief "experimental" outburst, Hans Andreus even took to writing sonnets again. Gerrit Kouwenaar was especially inspired by the more her-

metic French poets such as René Char and Henri Michaux. Bert
Schierbeek's texts showed traces of Kenneth Patchen but also
of the rural dialect native to the area where he grew up. Per-
sonal tensions within the group also began to surface, so that
by the end of the decade one could hardly speak of a "gener-
ation of the fifties." What was left was a clutch of gifted poets
each of whom proceeded to go his own way.

In Flanders, that other slice of Northwest Europe where
Dutch is spoken, the situation was quite different. Because
Flanders had not remained outside World War I as had the
Netherlands, "modern poetry" had infiltrated there much ear-
lier, in particular in the writings of Paul van Ostayen (1896–
1928), who can rightly be called the first truly modern poet in
Dutch. Along with Apollinaire's "calligrammes," it was Ger-
man Expressionism, which he encountered in Berlin just after
World War I, that brought Van Ostayen to a kind of poetry
that was totally revolutionary in Dutch.* Van Ostayen's friend
Gaston Burssens, born in the same year but granted a much
longer life (he died in 1965), was the nestor behind the Flemish
review *Tijd en Mens* (Time and Man), established in 1949. This
review, edited by the novelist Louis Paul Boon, the critic Jan
Walravens, and the poet-playwright-novelist Hugo Claus, was
an important phenomenon of postwar writing in Dutch. But
despite it there was no real breakthrough in Flanders as there
was in the North, and an attempt in 1952 at cooperation be-
tween the Flemish and the Dutch Experimentalists quickly came
to nothing. It was not until the late fifties and early sixties that
a really productive form of cooperation came about, in the re-
view *Gard Sivik* (Civic Guard), the mouthpiece of the "second
generation of Flemish Experimentalists" founded by Gust Gils,
Hugues C. Pernath, and Paul Snoek. Begun in 1955 as a purely
Flemish publication, *Gard Sivik* quickly attracted Dutch col-
laborators and eventually the editorial board became half-

---

*For poetry of Paul van Ostayen available in English, see his *Feasts of Fear and Agony*
(written 1918–1920), tr. Hidde Van Ameyden van Duym (New York: New Direc-
tions, 1976) and his *The First Book of Schmoll: Selected Poems 1920–1928*, tr. Theo Her-
mans, James S Holmes, and Peter Nijmeijer (Amsterdam: Bridges Books, 1982).

Flemish, half-Dutch. The Dutch influence continued to increase, particularly after a Dutch publisher took over the review, until by the time it died and came phoenixlike back to life as *De Nieuwe Stijl* (The New Style), the last Fleming had left the editorial board. This was also the last effort at achieving a single stream of poetry in Dutch. Since that time, the Dutch in the North and the Flemish in the South have gone their own ways, separated by a common language, and it can hardly be said that there is any real interaction, even though several of the leading Flemish authors, poets and novelists alike, are published by Dutch houses.

Poetry in Dutch had its beginnings at least as early as the twelfth century, and attained a peak in the seventeenth century with a group of poets whose glories, though hardly known abroad, fall but little short of those of their painting colleagues of the Dutch Golden Age. But that age was followed by a long period of drought in which there was hardly one poet of international quality or repute. Then, in the 1880s, a new generation of brilliant poets suddenly emerged, strongly inspired by the English Romantics, and Dutch poetry experienced its first resurgence in two hundred years. The creative genius of the Dutch has through the ages found its primary outlet in the art of painting, just as that of the English has expressed itself primarily through literature: the true Shakespeare of the Low Countries is a man named Rembrandt. Yet the Dutch also wrote, just as the English also painted, and in that writing the accent of the Dutch has for centuries been on poetry more than on fiction—and far more than on playwriting. One reason for this is no doubt that the Dutch were always more churchgoers than playgoers. The "revolution" of the "generation of the 1880s" was not coincidentally a rebellion against what was called "parson's poetry": upstanding, edifying rhymes in what all too often was a monotonous metrical drone. With the arrival of the generation of the eighties, poetry had once again become an adventure.

It was this spirit of adventure, largely gone from Dutch poetry by the 1930s, that the writers of the fifties introduced once more: the spirit that all things are possible, that there are whole new continents, worlds, galaxies even, to discover. Undoubtedly this new spirit had a great deal to do with the euphoria of liberation from five years of German oppression. Everything was allowed again, everything was possible—in poetry, as in life. It was a dream that was all too soon cruelly shattered, first by the Cold War, then by the Korean War, and what had seemed paradise became the domain of the serpent.

Meanwhile a new generation grew up, one that had experienced the war and the Occupation in a much less conscious way. This new generation did not have to deal with the dominance of a sterile school of writers driveling in traditional verse forms about the "simple pleasures," writers who had known nothing of Dadaism, Surrealism, Futurism, Imagism, Vorticism . . . all those great upheavals of twentieth-century European and American poetry that the Dutch writers of the fifties had incorporated into a new tradition. As Lucebert had written:

> the time of the one-sided movements is past
> that's why the poetry of experiment is a sea
> at the mouth of all those rivers
> we once gave names to like
> dada   (that's not a name)
> there we are then damp
> no one to pigeonhole

With the work of the Experimental generation, Dutch poetry had rejoined the modern international tradition, just as it had been lifted above provincialism seventy years earlier by the generation of the eighties. It was thus only natural that the influence of the group should gradually stir reactions. One of the most important representatives of the Experimentalists, Gerrit Kouwenaar, had formulated the aim of the group in this way:

In contrast to the traditional poets, the experimental poet does not impose his will on the word, but instead allows himself to be guided by the word. The poet must follow the word: the word transports him as he writes to unknown and yet now recognizable realms, and should obstacles appear, the poet does not hesitate to break up grammar, attack the rational-logical language of thought, and in every other way give the words in poems their own *sense*. Thus a poem does not express, is not a fancy straightjacket for some sleeping beauty, is not an imitated chunk of reality like a portrait or a still life, but is rather a self-contained piece of action, a compact ball of tensions, motivated by a conglomeration of causes and effects: sounds, rhythms, images, meanings, and their telescopic fishing-rod extensions. I don't mean to say that the experimental poem has no "purpose," but it is in fact more the purpose of the *poem* than that of the *poet,* who does not depict something that he had stored up ahead of time, but experiences something he had not known before.

Dutch poetry had changed, to use Tristan Tzara's terms, from being "poetry as a means of expression" to being "poetry as an activity of the spirit," from modesty to exuberance, often even flamboyance. With the result that it was in essence totally in conflict with the Dutch character, which is to a large extent determined by centuries of Calvinism. The backlash would not be long in coming.

The "new poetry" that was to challenge that of the Experimentalists emerged in the late fifties and early sixties around two publications: the magazine *Barbarber,* set up in 1958 by J. Bernlef and K. Schippers, and the review *Gard Sivik. Gard Sivik,* as several Dutch poets began to exert their influence on it around 1960 to the detriment of the original Flemish editors, turned ever more obviously toward a poetry that was in almost all ways opposed to the poetry of the fifties. In *Barbarber,* at the same time, ties were sought with American pop art and French "new realism." According to its subtitle, *Barbarber* was a "magazine of texts," and for the first time in Dutch writing no distinction was made between "poems," around which term an air of something "higher" inevitably still lingered, and "other texts": newspaper articles, shopping lists, pages from telephone books. In *Barbarber*'s pages, Dutch poetry was democratized: no one word was any "higher" or "better" than any other, and no one subject took precedence. There was at the same time a shift in foreign influences: Pound's *Cantos* gave way to William Carlos Williams' "I have eaten the plums/ that were in/ the icebox." And the found poem made its appearance: Armando jotted down train conversations and wrote an "Agrarian Cycle" constructed entirely from a pamphlet on farm machinery.

The name Armando became associated with *Gard Sivik,* which promoted a new poetry in a much more ordered way than *Barbarber. Barbarber* was an extremely whimsical journal that bore the strong impress of the "neo-Dadaist" poet Schippers. One spring, subscribers received an issue consisting entirely of wallpaper samples (spring is, after all, the time to repaper). Schippers was particularly interested in distinctions: whether there was any difference between a photograph of an etching and the photograph of a photograph of an etching, or whether, when the weather has been quite a bit above freezing for several weeks, you could still talk about a "thaw." What he was looking for was "a new alphabet of reality"; what he found was a new way of seeing. *Barbarber* introduced the undramatic into poetry: for Schippers a blacked-out house was "war" just as much as a house hit by a bomb, the delivery of a can of tomato soup to his lady just as much an expression of "love" as a close embrace.

But while *Barbarber* never turned its back on the generation of the fifties, *Gard Sivik / De Nieuwe Stijl* did so more and more. Indeed, *Gard Sivik,* in its final issue, bore as a subheading "a new date in poetry." Where the writers of the fifties had been closely allied to the painters of the group called Cobra, based in Copenhagen, Brussels, and Amsterdam, among them Karel Appel, Constant, Corneille, and the poet-painter Lucebert, the poets of the "new style" worked closely with the visual artists in the Zero group, of which the poet-painter Armando was an important representative. The theories on which these poets and painters based their work were best stated by Zero spokesman Jan Schoonhoven, who wrote in 1965:

Zero is first and foremost a new conception of reality, in which the individual role of the artist is kept to a minimum. The Zero artist merely selects, isolates parts of reality (materials as well as ideas stemming from reality) and exhibits them in the most neutral way. The avoidance of personal feelings is essential to Zero . . . Zero's method is determined by its point of departure. Zero does not intend to create a new form. The form is given in advance by the reality isolated. The aim is to ground reality as art in an impersonal way.

This statement is the complete antithesis of the one by Kouwenaar outlining the aim of the Experimental group ten years earlier. It might be said that the poets of the fifties wanted to write poetry with a maximum of means and those of the sixties with a minimum, that for the poets of the fifties what counted was how much they could get into a poem, and for those of the sixties how much they could leave out. For a long time Dutch poetry oscillated between these two poles.

Even when a particular poetic persuasion dominates the literary scene, it goes without saying that there are always a great many poets who refuse to be part of a group, a trend, or a school. Writing poetry is a highly individual matter, and the Dutch are by nature individualists who chafe when not allowed to go their own way. The chief characteristic of poetry in Dutch from the mid-sixties on is its diversity. The concept of "programmatic" poetry can be used only for the writings of a handful of poets such as H. C. ten Berge and Hans Faverey, who, following in Kouwenaar's footsteps, aspire to create totally autonomous linguistic structures. The poets occasionally referred to as the "Tirade Group"—Judith Herzberg, Hanny Michaelis, Rutger Kopland, and their associates—had little in common except that they usually published in the same literary review, *Tirade*.

The second and final issue of *De Nieuwe Stijl* appeared in 1966; *Barbarber* went on until 1971, but by that time its impact had long diminished. Since then there has been no new, clear mainstream. Nor is that surprising. There is a similar situation in the international world of painting, where many artists are busy doing their own thing, and often doing it very well, but without the slightest indication of anything like an *élan* from an avant-garde. It is almost as if everyone everywhere had to catch his breath after all the incredible changes in art and poetry alike during the first sixty years of the century. On top of this there is, of course, most certainly in Europe, the ever-present threat of nuclear annihilation. With total destruction staring you in the face, your mind is not on artistic manifestos.

It is striking all the same that during the past few years in the Netherlands (though not yet in Flanders) a number of younger poets, among them Jan Kuijper, are once again making exclusive use of the sonnet—that form so jeered at by the poets of the fifties (Lucebert wrote "a sonnet to end all sonnets": "I/ me/ me/ I// I/ me/ me/ I// I/ me/ mine// I/ me/ mine") and so strictly taboo for at least a quarter of a century. Other poets also have moved or are moving away from free verse and back to metrical norms and stanzaic rhyming patterns. It would almost seem that for these poets, of whom Gerrit Komrij is the most significant, the work of the generation of the fifties hardly exists but to be rebelled against. They, and Komrij in particular, are reaching back instead to nineteenth-century poets who, with rare exceptions, had long been considered utterly uninteresting and trivial. In 1979 Komrij compiled a huge anthology of nineteenth- and twentieth-century Dutch poetry which demonstrated by startling examples that attitudes to nineteenth-century poetry needed to be reconsidered. Dealing summarily with all the poets of the fifties except Lucebert, the book was a direct attack on the Experimental generation. In his introduction Komrij challenged

the way in which Dutch poetry is always being anthologized: as if poetry is pre-eminently the domain of emotional expression, lofty moods, flying colors, and bombast. The bread is always cut the same way, whether it is done with an ethical or a political knife. I wanted to present a different slice: poems that sharpen and entertain one's reason (without turning reason into a religion once more). The accent here lies, roughly speaking, more on craft and taste and mature insight than on stammering or mundane sentiments or being simple, more on satire, masquerade, and distancing than on deadly seriousness, single-mindedness, or life at its fullest. Something like that.

Of the "freedom from the ordinary logic of sequence, jump-
ing from one image to the next by 'association' rather than by
the usual cause-effect route," so central to Rodman's "moder-
nity" and at the very heart of most writing of the fifties, of all
that nothing remains.

New directions in the arts are always unexpected, and so it
would seem that in Dutch poetry the eighties will probably
produce another breakthrough in some still unclear direction.
On the one hand, there are a number of performance-oriented
poets, for whom an unusual way of delivering a text in public
is at least as important as the text itself. The shining example
of this group, for years relegated to the subculture by the of-
ficial critics, is the work of the Beat Generation, particularly
that of Allen Ginsberg, as introduced to the Dutch by way of
Simon Vinkenoog's translations and his own latter-day Gins-
berg-like verse. On the other hand, at the more official level,
the level that makes its way into literary histories, the "enter-
tainment" element so strong in the work of many writers of
the sixties, including my own (so much so that Remco Cam-
pert once sighed, "since buddingh'/ many people expect/ of
poetry/ an evening full of laughs")—this element would seem
to be fading.

It would be a pity if it disappeared entirely, although it must
be admitted that these days there are not many reasons for us
Europeans to laugh. The worsening economic situation con-
stitutes another, new threat to Dutch poetry, as to poetry
everywhere, or at least to poetry in the West: publishers are
finding themselves in a critical situation, so that it is becoming
more difficult than ever for young poets—and many older ones
as well—to get their work published. In the early thirties, the
foremost younger poet in the Netherlands, Hendrik Marsman,
lamented: "Countrymen, I shall sink if my song cannot be
heard." Then, at least, he could get that desperate cry into print.
Today that is not always possible.

CEES BUDDINGH'

1945–1950:
PRELUDE TO
EXPERIMENT

And in my life the poem revealed,
in which you dance . . .
   —GERRIT ACHTERBERG, "Ravel's Bolero"

. . . it was only love that could make
the pencil move in my dreams
when I fell asleep on what seems
this poem now . . .
   —LEO VROMAN, "To Whom This May Concern"

Pierre Kemp
(1886–1967)

KARMA

Then I was young
and every woman a hell
painted in pastel.
Now I am wise
and no two women ever
are in one paradise.

(translated by Fred van Leeuwen)

HONEYSUCKLE YELLOW

Wedded to a redolence
a honeying color cast with care
its fragrant arms round the expanse
of the dear, familiar air.
I carried my nose repeatedly past,
once there, once back, and once again,
with all the grief of crazy gentlemen,
sighing that summer does not last.

(translated by Fred van Leeuwen)

LIFE SENTENCE

We arrived and were naked and bare,
like an animal or a flower.
Then we were taught the use of underwear
and after that the hour.
We went to the Sun for our education
with ferro-concrete as our concentration.
Flowers we picked for our dearest sorrows,
praising truth, goodness, and beauty in chorus.
And if we undress after many tomorrows,
a plateful of stars will be waiting for us.

(translated by Fred van Leeuwen)

GAMBLE ON RED

The flag of a different poem flies
from either side of my eyes.
On the side of my heart waves the Red of the Living.
On the side of my liver the Black of the Dead
and the problem of taking and giving;
I keep gambling, though, on the Red.

(translated by Fred van Leeuwen)

Gerrit Achterberg
(1905–1962)

GRIEF

Grief, I deny
the sun its light,
the seer his sight,
this universe its balance, weight,
death the right
to any writ
to take her from my side.

Avoid me not, but lay
eternity's robe in readiness:

I lie in the dark, her counterpart,
but for my breath, but for my heart.

(translated by James Brockway)

WORD

You are laid low with soil and stones,
rain has entered into you,
the snow become a part of you,
winds lay bare your bones.

The light in your eyes continues to shine,
as though today you had waked they stare,
yet they follow sun nor moon,
touch no star.

As far as my blood's concerned, you are
with every element
requited and replete.

Yet somewhere a word must lie that is
your perfect counterfeit.

(translated by James Brockway)

RAVEL'S BOLERO

Above this limitless morass:
blue-brilliant bird, approaching, gone.

In the eternal wilderness;
o, caravan.

Across the sea a ship, alone,
horizon out, horizon in.

And in my life the poem revealed,
in which you dance with eyelids sealed.

(translated by James Brockway)

HOUSE

House, I still inhabit you.
In my mind your lamps burn on
as though my mind and you were one:
time nor distance cannot strew
their intervening shadows in
between the light of now and then.

Dark, your objects gleam in me,
heavy with eternity:
death can differ no whit from this
except that here I still possess
the time in which it settles down,
becomes a poem.

(translated by James Brockway)

LULLABY

In my memory you flare
like summer lightning in the night.
I see a landscape of despair
lit in a second's light.

Now every circuit is complete.
My loaded arms hang down like stones.
The summer lightning draws its sheet
over your bones.

(translated by James Brockway)

SLEEPWALKING

Last night I walked with you again
down the muffled avenues of sleep,
and now that morning has returned
nothing has changed:
except that two, who in the night were one,
were joined together utterly,
have left me here alone now day is come,
and, arm in arm, go walking on.

(translated by James Brockway)

SKIN

Time folds you in,
and I spread wide
around you with my sanctified
linen of immortality.
No death can begin
in this new skin.

(translated by James S Holmes)

STATUE

A body, blind with sleep,
stands up in my arms.
Its heaviness weighs on me.
Death-doll.
I'm an eternity too late.
And where's your heartbeat?

The thick night glues us together,
makes us compact with each other.
"For God's sake go on holding me—
my knees are broken,"
you mumble against my heart.

It's as if I held up the earth.
And slowly, moss is creeping
all over our two figures.

(translated by Adrienne Rich)

TABLEAU MOURANT

We're standing on a stage.
We cannot disappear,
since one of us is dead
and bans the other's fear.

The curtains of the stage
are forever twilight red.

The sun shines still.
The trees grow tall.
How much we would diminish
if either moved at all.

(translated by James S Holmes)

BRIDEGROOM

The morning road's fogged in. My cycle speeds
onward and onward into one same gray.
Behind me follows a sheer wall of mist.
Roadbed and shoulder can only be guessed.
I am a darker groove through these fresh halls
of brand-new metal murmuring
with soft seas in my ear, and bear
a deep strip of surprise into the still
dowry of morning. Lo, the bridegroom comes.

(translated by James S Holmes)

ICHTHYOLOGY

They've found a coelacanthus in the sea,
the missing link between two kinds of fish.
The finder wept, at its discovery,
in wonderment. The age-long broken chain

lay for the first time closed beneath his eyes.
And everyone who stood around the fish
felt at that moment quite consumed by all
the thousand thousand years that stretched behind.

Order from man down to the dinosaur,
and from the dinosaur deep into dust,
further than all our instruments can reach.

Aware of this, we may pretend as though
the order upwards is the same, and so
be able to look in on God at lunch.

(translated by James S Holmes)

ACCOUNTABILITY

Old oblivion-book, that I lay open.
White eye-corner rounding the page.

Gold lace slips out under the evening,
Green animals creep backwards.

Lifelessness of the experimental station.
Added-up, subtracted sum.

Black night. Over the starlight skims
God's index finger, turning the page.

Death comes walking on all fours
past the room, a crystal egg,

with the lamp, the books, the bread,
where you are living and life-size.

(translated by Adrienne Rich)

BALLAD OF THE STORE CLERK

I
A young man's lying in the sky, stretched out,
flat on his back. He holds his arms up tight
against his body, as if it would break.
The moon-barge floats and rolls above his eyes.

The evening's peace reverberates from him
the way he drifts there in the Sunday suit
he was supplied with by a clothing store.
He doesn't move one yard, ahead or back.

We, far beneath him, cycle on towards home;
we switch the light on and sit down and read.
Somehow I feel he'll still be there: alone,

ethereal, exalted, dead and pure.
He was a clerk in a Terneuzen store,
at P. de Gruyter's or at Albert Heijn's.

II
"You shouldn't spoil him," said my wife. "That he's
clerk in a store is more than you can say.
That, let alone De Gruyter's. They could lodge
a court complaint against you for bad faith."

To prove my case I pointed out his wife,
searching in desperation whether he
might still turn up. They have already dredged,
and called out the entire civilian defence.

"Well then," she said, "I want him to be found:
you bring him slowly back where he belongs,
gently and walking in his sleep and well.

Then when his wife comes home she'll hurriedly
set the alarm clock, and from that hour on
the old good life will go on as before."

III
She wanted the impossible. You can't
embroider on an image as you like.
There's more already than it can endure
in the associations it begets.

Just now he came within a single hair
of being back there, growing bitterer
year after year amidst the figs and jams
meted and measured out in countless pounds.

We looked outside. He lay decaying in
the sweetness of the myriads of stars.
The nebulae gave him a leprous look.

Milky ways washed through him, and at last
we could no longer make him out at all:
quivering towards us came the firmament.

.   .   .   .

They bring his clothing back from the police,
covered with ants and eaten out by molds.
He was buried at once, as black as soot.

.   .   .   .

"He's standing shaving in the looking-glass.
His wife is hurrying to pack his lunch,
since Monday is an early day for him."

(translated by James S Holmes)

Terneuzen is a small town in Zeelandish Flanders, the narrow strip of Flanders along
the south bank of the Scheldt that belongs to the Netherlands. P. de Gruyter and Al-
bert Heijn were at the time two leading Dutch chain grocery stores.—Translator's Note.

Leo Vroman
(1915–   )

TO WHOM THIS MAY CONCERN

A host of printed letters I can offer
but look: no mouth, and I can't proffer
my hot hand through this paper; what can I do?
I cannot reach you.

If I could comfort you, I'd weep,
so lay your hand upon this paper, it's my skin;
ease this fierce fossilization of the words;
take them warm within.

For most of you, all I wrote
may have remained too remote.
And for others, too painfully close.
I have still only love for those,

as it was only love that could make
the pencil move in my dreams
when I fell asleep on what seems
this poem now—so read it awake
as if I were under this page,
as if barred by these lines I could feel
your pain reach into my cage
to have and to heal.

If you wake up this text you had better
know that it sleeps in the nude.
Embarrass it with a light touch

and read it like a late letter.
No love is ever crude
and it loves you so much.

(translated by the author and Peter Nijmeijer)

INDIAN SUMMER

During dinner, out on the balcony,
and drinking in long drafts,
I suddenly seem to have tumbled
through a hole in my memory

and I leave my water tumbler standing;
it won't even return to my hand,
now that I think of the ocean
between me and my motherland.

So bitterly full of water, so dingy
that the dolphins and the dead
vanish like things in a jungle,
choking with depth and cold.

Sometimes I dreamingly feel
my slithering way down through it.
But the only thing heard of the land
I ask about is cold eel,

for Holland is dark and tiny.
A single pale pink queen
can only just fit inside it—
if she has a short enough train.

To talk is to puff in someone's face;
to gesture is to give someone a cuff.
People start at the sound of a laugh,
confusing proximity with hate.

No, even groping for heath and strand
(and though I may close my ear
to hear Holland's storms) still I fear
I'd rather have homesickness than Holland.

I wade through this strange and eerie
relaxing easiest of all
on this broad and endless island
under attack by fall,
where the spring of death has begun.
The parks here are utterly filled
with trees and trees that are gilded
red like big, leafy suns.
The leaves slowly burn dead
in lazily smoking red fires;
the afternoon hours are slow
and the sun boils low and red.

Sweet girls who do not know
how gently they are decaying
stroll in blue jeans, they perspire
and turn red from the gradual dying
of the rusting light on their cheeks,
and the sons of Persians and Greeks
walk with their hair on fire,
pushed along by desire
beneath the falling leaves
that swish through the air like breathing.

The snow-white houses veined
by the shadows of boughs are already
visible. Winter is on the way.

Come, I get up, it's turning chilly,
though dusk is still far off; I put
my glass on top of my plate
and go inside and push the door shut.

(translated by James S Holmes)

FEATHERS

Women have twisted wings,
they sadly finger their sky.
Where chickens would smilingly fly
they sit and flutter at things.

When their withered feathers fall
cold makes women think
and sadnesses cover us all
and feathers, scented with pink.

Bald wings revealing old skin
are tender to behold
as the ivory membranes unfold
with a spray of fishbones within,
when the aged women die
and soar like blushing bats
clad in coats and battered hats
to obliterate the sky.

(written in English)

THE HORSE OF DEATH

I was roused this morning in May
by the ping of an armchair spring,
as if a beast shifted this way and that way
in it, while heavily sitting.

So I made for this chair, in that room,
and a horse had the back of its head
turned at me, tall, and sad,
unkempt, and full of doom.

Speech failing me, I tried
to push the thing in its chair
doorward, but the touch of its hide
and its girlishly fragrant hair

filled me with such gentle hate,
called love by so many a brave
that I thought it had come to mate
or to be my unwieldy slave.

I buried my face in its chest,
as its arms, too old for me,
forced me tightly to rest,
more and more tightly.

I screamed, I slapped its face
and burst from its embrace.
Now, never to be its friend,
I can never walk by its side,
whispering, hand in hand,
though once this horse I must ride,
though Time rubberized its toes,
and cotton rolls from its hide,
berries bleed where it goes.

Into where ever branches I flee
its neck smells thinly at me,
and observed by the whites of its eyes
I shrink back among leaves and vines,
feeling my hairs rise, my tears rise,
and my spines.

(written in English)

DAILY PREPARATIONS

Often, before I come home, I see
blood under the door, looking at me,
and then her head from under our bed
dying, dying repeatedly.

Sometimes I call home,
and the phone does not answer,
indicating my family
has been squashed, a mesh of flesh and bone
against one wall,
wood splintered, the TV set
crushed, but happily playing yet,
and there, burping in an armchair,
sits a tremendous ball of hair.

At other times, I must confess,
anxiety corrupts me less,
and at best one fire or a fetid guest
await me and my carelessness.
Then merely living will suffice
to balance last night's blessing twice.
Especially when it smells or snows,
I sneeze too much or taste like prose,

then by all rights I need not add
fear to my fate, stay blood unspilled,
and finding as much as one child killed
would make me so mad.

(written in English)

FEBRUARY

This year's ice age is half gone,
spring impossible, autumn erased,
the stoneware country thickly glazed
a plate I rarely walk upon
as I do today, but all you can hear
is my collar, rubbing my hard-edged ear.

The sun rises like a blinding moon.
No one sees and finds no one.
At noon a frightened greyhound
runs the extended shadow
of a hunchback deer
across the whitewashed ground.
How lonely the sun must persevere.
You can sense it strain down here
and yet it must shine another month
before the earth turns drunk.

This month has shrunk with cold.
Yet over congealing days piled thin
must wave some lukewarm haze.
Quite soon it will be mild.

It refuses to snow in my past.
Rarely I remember a patch
of hometown street on white
where I scratched the frost off a pane.
A view gladly lost. There, I see
the heavy green of an elm tree
come to the curtains again. It falls.

Still, there is one tremendous thing
sometimes darkening the window
that can drag out a memory
of thick and whispering snow.
That was the monstrous, wild,
black horse sleigh;
like a blanket of night it would pass
plumaged by the frost-feathered glass,
soundlessly except that time

I was allowed out, on the steps
and I heard a soft hiss, then chimes,
tiny jingles, creaking rigs—
there! The black horse, a hundred feet tall
and then that gold-trimmed house
topped by a multigloved wig
moved by like a ship.

All things, just a few winters old,
displayed themselves still from below;
but even then, this month was too cold
for other wonders to grow in.

(translated by the author and Peter Nijmeijer)

Adriaan Morriën
(1912–   )

GASTRONOMY

She is the finest banquet you could eat:
from top to toe fried liver, beefsteak, kidneys,
sweet & sour like a none-too-large gherkin,
a salad with olive oil, wine vinegar,
the smell of garlic, fish fried in finest oils;
her rump is strongly peppered, and her sex
drips honey and is slightly, deliciously sticky.
You can eat yourself ill on her, you drink
from her body as from a heavenly drinking glass,
and when you're tired you lie still nibbling at her,
careful not to interrupt this stream
that flows from her and permeates through you
to your remotest fibers, where you are
not human but a stone that's learning to drink and eat.

(translated by James S Holmes)

SHIPWRECK

Her breasts stormed out in front of her,
nippled cyclones,

her lap foamed like a sea
and I was shipwrecked on her coast.

I walked ashore on her and everything was unfamiliar:
the strangers who gave me hot rum to drink,
the small wooden room with the view of the harbor,
the sea which had laid itself to rest,
lighthouse, semaphore and even a fort
which wrapped itself in silence,
the silence after a last shot.

This is my father, she laughed.
A gray man looked at me piercingly.

And this my mother.
A much too decided woman
asked the ins and outs of me,
then mended my clothes, which were in rags,
and put me near the fire to dry.

But later we fled.

In the dunes she knew the places where you could descend
to the depth of each other's body.
Space had a big sense of its own dignity.
I kissed her in places where
I'd never before been able
to kiss a woman washed ashore
because I had never wanted to bend down:
between her panties and her stocking,
the pathway to lap and ass
so angelically sweet
that it makes me just as mystical
as at my mother's apron
when I still reached to heaven with my forehead
in smells of urine
elastic
and starch.

And therefore she laughed at me
as if I were the child and not she,
but lay down willingly
under my lips
against my skin.

Between my teeth I carried her home.

(translated by Ria Leigh-Loohuizen)

MY PARENTS' HOUSE

Language was used sparingly:
caresses had to be stolen.
When my mother stroked me she was ashamed
and I was ashamed—our shames were still separate.

I loved the scissors she cut with,
her thimble, the thread she moistened,
the whirring of the sewing machine
and the silence when the machine was still.

She slept in a matchless bed
and when my father got up for work
I took his place in her warmth.

I touched her as another child
touches the wall it sleeps against
with life-size fingertips
and without the wall noticing.

(translated by Ria Leigh-Loohuizen)

THE USE OF A WALL MIRROR

Alone at home, naked on my bed,
I hold the mirror out of my parents' bedroom
above me and support it with my left hand,
while I masturbate with my right.

I look at the reflection of my white skin,
my thin arms, my long legs,
and my tanned face, a boy's face still, with spectacles.

Only halfway infatuated with myself
I try to recognize in me
reflection and lover:
I'd rather be lying in a girl's arms.

My eyes examine myself: I'm not ashamed.
There is no cause to lose myself in my gaze.

I listen to the silence in the house,
the single silence I trust.

Words emerge, as in someone fleeing mortally afraid,
without a context and unforgettable.

It's hard to hold the mirror still
and not relax the movement of
my right hand: a regularity
that I must keep in hand,
trained on other afternoons alone at home,
or before going to sleep
while I thought about a girl
or preferably a dozen girls
I married in lightning succession.

A pianist, too, doesn't just fall from heaven.

(translated by James S Holmes)

Hans Lodeizen
(1924–1950)

EVENING AT THE MERRILLS

they lie on mattresses
longing for a chair
as five o'clock approaches and
the cocktails are ready.

this they think to themselves
is the afternoon as the little
gramophone churns out Stravinsky
or la Petite Suite by Roussel.

Madame arrives back home outside
it's cold the show was *marvelous*

are the guests no the guests haven't
arrived yet here's the newspaper.

they wait for the afternoon to end
the afternoon itself would rather be evening
here are the guests take off your coats
kiss on the cheek, *darling*.
Oh good, the cocktails are ready.

there the world is visible as though
seen through spectacle lenses obliquely
or like an olive in a little glass

they hover in the air
they laugh their glasses empty
the clock tinkles with laughter the opera
was *absolutely divine*

he stayed for a week at Gide's
and she went on a cruise with Cocteau
when he shows you things
the moon is buried beneath flowers

oh look, those white clouds there against
the mountain they're not clouds they're
white doves swarming around a coach

and are the cocktails milder . . .

(translated by James Brockway)

The Merrills are the parents of James Merrill, the American poet, who at the time was in college at Amherst together with Hans Lodeizen; the setting is their Manhattan apartment.—Editors' Note.

JIM I WOULD LIKE TO KNOW

Jim I would like to know
what makes it worthwhile
for you to keep on writing
letters, essays, and poems
in which you recommend the world
and weigh her like an expert merchant.
how come you never
tire and shut your eyes and
think I wish they'd all go
to hell with their idle
gossip and keep on writing
letters, essays, and poems

from which I recognize you and
through which I meet you laughing
and telling me to keep faith
for I am very tired and as
I speak hope flows out of me.
Jim what makes it worthwhile
for you to keep on writing
letters, essays, and poems . . . etc.

(translated by Peter Nijmeijer)

Jim is James Merrill.—Editors' Note.

LA VOIX DU PEUPLE

we want to be amused,
to be divinely amused
by the night wind and its elegant
odors (invisible princesses)
by the piccolo of the bats and the
violin of the ugly black beetles
we want to be amused.

we want to laugh amid the dying
blue in the sky and my aunt
the nightingale sings from a droning throat
we want to spread out our chairs
on the terrace, the wine tinkling
in the glasses, the girls and their high
thin voices. we want to laugh.

we want to have fun in white
icebergs of sheets and bowl away
the stealthy eyes from the sky and

be drunk on bare feet oh the contact
between hands and the buzz
of the voice between the dried lips
in the night. we want to have fun.

(translated by James S Holmes)

DISHONORABLE SEAMAN'S GRAVE

several minutes each day I manage
to flee into a new world
where there's no need for sighs and there is
no voice at my back although I know
I have to return but I don't cry.

if I could only stay in that world a
little bit longer and every day
longer until I dream of the
ordinary world now and then like a
child having nightmares at night,

but no longer able to believe in it,
because I have something more worthwhile,
have found a treasure that no one
believed in, gold at the bottom of the sea
from a sunken ship no one knew of it

and then my happiness will be like
the glory of that wreck, a darker
shadow rocking on the ocean floor
a grave for stouthearted sailors whose
gold adorns their bodies like a lamp.

(translated by James S Holmes)

"AN EMPTY MAILMAN DROWNS IN THE COUNTRY ROAD"

for Adriaan Morriën

dammit it's almost fall again
and my tired body that knows no honey
body weak to extremes and torn
it's like an old house in Greenwich Village

the trees almost ready to pack in their wares
their leaves into the suitcases of the soil
the wind's a fleet key and across
the lid it spreads a cloth of clouds

my body's windows are blind and by
the open fire of my dreams i see
the days playing tag like flames and disappearing
in an old treetrunk of the house

what time is it getting to be the rivers
wiggle their hips like a window against the landscape
my body my tender body slowly leaving
or an empty mailman drowns in the country road.

(translated by James S Holmes)

HE WAS THE BEST OF ALL

he was the best of all
i lived in him

he was a light house
that wore geraniums in the mornings.

(the night in him was a scent
a breath of wind)

i shall hunt down his footsteps
in the world and follow them
shadow his ghost,
catch it one night (beside
a wood the path goes along
the edge between the bushes)
and marry him by
the light of a town
in the distance. then i shall
gaily go down along crooked
paths and drown
in the city's sidewalks
(thoughtless, happy)

(translated by James S Holmes)

THE WORLD AN OLD MUSIC BOX

the world an old music box that must sing

the dancer it is his body that sings
the writer it is his life that sings
the musician his head
the poet his throat
and the sculptor his fingers that sing in the stone
it is the world that sings

the world an old music box

but the lovers sing too their bodies sing
from the world the whole world a song ascends

into the night the sick man sends the guitar of his longing
and the lonely child plays on his body as on a guitar
(in the afternoon a sad song rises between his fingers)
the exhausted travelers too sing in train or omnibus
and the murderer sings with the knife in his fingers
and the thief sings with the beads in his hand
(and the sailor sings in bed with a tango).

(translated by James Brockway)

THE FIFTIES:
THE EXPERIMENTAL
REVOLT

. . . rime-rats, jeer,
jeer at this much too lovely school of verse.
   —LUCEBERT, "School of Poetry"

I try in poetic fashion
that is to say
simplicities luminous waters
to give expression to
the expanse of life at its fullest . . .
   —LUCEBERT, "I Try in Poetic Fashion"

Or take the surf. Beaten to bits
on the rocks but not beaten,
resumes the assault and thus is poetry.
   —REMCO CAMPERT, "Poetry Is an Act"

Poetry, cruel machine . . .
   —PAUL RODENKO, "Robot Poetry"

. . . the word the wonder of the world . . .
   —HANS ANDREUS, "I Spoke the Words of the World"

Lucebert
(1924–   )

SCHOOL OF POETRY

I'm not some lovable rime-spook
I am the expeditious crook
of love, see the hate underneath
and upon it a cackling deed.

lyrics are the parents of politics,
I'm merely the reporter of revolt
and my mysticism is the spoilt
lie-fodder virtue swallows when it's sick.

I announce that the velvet poets
are shyly and humanistically dying.
henceforth the impassioned torturers, vying
musically, shall swell their hot iron throats.

and I, who live in this book of verse
like a rat in a trap, long for the sewer
of revolution and roar: rime-rats, jeer,
jeer at this much too lovely school of verse.

(translated by James S Holmes)

I TRY IN POETIC FASHION

I try in poetic fashion
that is to say
simplicities luminous waters
to give expression to
the expanse of life at its fullest

if I had not been a man
like masses of men
but if I had been who I was
the stone or fluid angel
birth and decay would not have touched me
the road from forlornness to communion
the stones stones beasts beasts birds birds road
would not be so befouled
as it can be seen to be in my poems
that are snapshots of that road

in this age what was always called
beauty beauty has burnt her face
she no longer comforts man
she comforts the larvae the reptiles the rats
but she startles man
and strikes him with the awareness
of being a breadcrumb on the universe's skirt

no longer evil alone
the deathblow alone makes us rebellious or meek
but also good
the embrace that leaves us fumbling in despair
at space

and so I sought out
language in her beauty
heard there she had nothing human left

but the speech defects of the shadow
but those of the earsplitting sunlight

(translated by James S Holmes)

SLOWLY I BEGIN TO PLAY THE GAME

slowly i begin to play the game of ancient kings:

opir who forgot about his people
after only three yards of wine
after two yards of wine
stored all his treasures in the belly
of the sea

hassall lover of spiced gingerbread
who sacrificed his life for even more delicate spices
and laid his strong lips
his stronger lips a thousand miles
in all directions and neglected
the celebrated bakers of his people

hikkim sun of mussah
who as a child hid inauspiciously
behind all the women's fans
listen 3 days after coronation
he vanished with the lowest of whores
vanished into the mists of the hills
. . . his golden rings lay with the jewish vendors

it's all the same story with the great ones
a million dusty lips
have said and sung this

but naitta the first and last queen
naitta hated the daylight
at dusk she wrote
the 700 unsurpassable rules of reigning
and died as a living stone

(translated by Peter Nijmeijer)

THE TIRED LOVERS THEY ARE MACHINES

the tired lovers they are machines
dancing mouse-still in transparent chambers
forging their invisible airship
out of oil mire and steaming water

long-drawn instruments laboriously shuffle
laboriously through thickly greased body
toward the hollow drained body

big sunny eyes
are fired off at heart level

this goes very silently this goes on naked feet
willpower wanders about in cold mantles
this goes very far this goes on sleeping wings

(translated by Peter Nijmeijer)

THE GREAT WALL

Ts'in Chi Huang Ti (Divus Augustus) who
had banned the scholars had burnt their books
who quaked before the constellations commanded

"destroy the land of the barbarians and build
round the realm a wall 10,000 miles long"

Ti Ling had left his wife alone for a day
to fetch the big wood for the approaching winter
home again sighing beneath a thousand branches
found only soldiers dancing on the burnt roof

General Mong T'ien with 300,000 men
defeated the barbarians and built the great wall
behind his high windows smiles the first man of Ts'in
he'll never know how soon destruction will come
to his own house

(translated by James S Holmes)

DEATH OF THE LORD OF THE FLIES

I kiss the notorious fly
who can spoil mountains
and name him beelzebub

at his command I feed
ten thousand devils
my atmosphere is
both a stall and a grave
he dances in his poison chair
golden braids around his gut
befoul the sun the glasses through which
he sees stars rise and fall in rhythm
he controls the universe and me
with his boorish buzz

no clock has ever tamely beaten me
no firewater has doused me

no savior made me miserable
but flies' omnipotence has bored into me
he spills good and bad
with his flamboyant trunk
near the trough of my body

I lie in ambush
suddenly with today's newspaper
I shatter the soulfeaster

(translated by Larry Ten Harmsel)

9000 JACKALS SWIMMING TO BOSTON

on every slave a pigeon loft to kick in the light of his decline
on every urethra a priest
on every vagina a father
bridges of academic blood
borne by too sudden heartbeats

this is anger
: to possess a voice in a torrent of embraces
to go boating on a long slow river in an underworld's lum-
        bering cesspool
to know for certain this world stinks
stinks under a smelly angel
an angel in silk stockings and with a fine writer's hand
who records only clamor
scores of sucklings
libretti of the blissful malicious and
études of octogenarians
: the noise of a world groaning under a pile of crossbeams

the angel
that rams down the urine barrels with wholesale judges
brigadiers bank messengers

yes
with the stake
the angel
that rams down all the pillars
of state

now in his service are contingents of
impromptu blacksmiths and poets who bare
the subterranean tree
who denude the tangled branches of chastity standing on
      stilts
the chastity that climbs like ivy and peeps in everywhere
that bores its thorny eyes into all and everything
buried under a blade let valid pennies bleed to death
because this stinks
because this counts
because this tastes nice
slobbering down to the *ding an sich*
d
  o
    w
      n
        t
          o
            t
              h
                e navel-floor of the effigy
the effigy rattling through a hollow universe
rattling with sacks full of mandatories
pursuing the chase
chasing the flight of these stoic (yet dressed in worsted mit-
      tens)

jackals
        possessing boston
9000   jackals
                swimming to boston
the borobudur of the bourgeoisie

(translated by Peter Nijmeijer)

BREYTEN BREYTENBACH MAY LOOK AT THE MOON

1
A faceless pig grunted far away
and today the news came
that your cell, sealed for two years,
was granted a thin mattress and a bit of moon

This poem is ashamed to be a poem
fury should be armed with more than words
this is indeed ashamed to be a poem, poet,
and not a jailer-killing slug

2
Under a storm of blows
they've made a crumpled raincoat
of your body
And now, for a place to dump the thing
after a long rainy season, you get a mattress
Ah—their ways get nicer all the time
now they offer you a slice of moon
like a crust that a careless mother
flings at her skinny kid
But they're still waiting for the nicest thing of all
for you to write a thankful ode
to your sluggish would-be killers

3
Pain cannot be measured
there will be days enduring like years
and minutes that surge
like the open sea

Seconds like crowds of gaping mouths
that might yet swallow the moon's blade
memories kindling like flames in your eyes
like shimmering fire at dusk

An old disaster, poet, you see it all ablaze
even small children must give up guitars
their agile fingers withered in screams
suffering, poet, you have seen quite enough

You have seen the far distant past
when a pale spirit declared himself god
his ghostly gray was not quite enough
so he called himself good and the white man's god

(translated by Larry Ten Harmsel)

Breyten Breytenbach is a South African poet and painter who at the time of writing
was serving a long sentence in prison for his activities against the present racist regime
in the country.—Editors' Note.

THE INDIGO EATER

Clouds like wolves above the roasted mountains
and in my dark room the table sagging
with the grapes in the valley with the crocks
full of tardy tears and on the horizon
socialism fades: meager fruit of often fasting

All I have to do is walk to the open window
a diamond mouth breathed upon by the moon

to be sure to get sleepless hands from the power
to demolish masks in attics and the jubilant
tremolo of overproduction: the fatal fountain

Nothing has purified me I heard the paralytic
whisper: do not touch me when I die
and behind the golden curtains of morning
the slight cries of the brides between rapacity
and the reception with much flesh: the gospel

For sure there is still a lot to weigh
lion or bouncer with knots in the eyes
and underbrush up the ass you're well disguised
or snowed-in high on the roof with some panhandled light
but the inevitable hurricane of delights the future
is easygoing is ready to explode in your face

(translated by Scott Rollins)

Gerrit Kouwenaar
(1923–   )

ELBA

for constant

I wear a warning bloodcoat
and I stand on elba.
My name is napoleon, among others my name is napoleon
and I stand on elba.
I bear a hundred names
and I stand on elba.
I am the other side of a gentleman.
My dear generals, look at my beak
on elba.
Walk with me the parks of doubt and exile.
There are nights I sit up and beg like a beaked dog.
My rock is brown, as you can see.
My eye is the clockwork of your inventions:
atom bomb! Thank you, gentlemen!

But now that terror dwells in paris
on the cobblestones still tasting of my parades,
in the sidewalk cafés of colonel sartre,
out of the sea I profess the eiffel tower,
steel affiliation of fear
on elba.

You think I'm dead?
I stand here with saber, beak, bloodcoat.
My body is big and fat
and fat with the bones of hitler and bismarck and nietzsche
and truman.
Chaplin is my lackey, but this I know:
he steals epaulettes for the fair
and tobacco for the slaves of soho,
he steals my history for marx—
generals, protest!

I stand like a cesspool on elba.
Oh generals, taste the lyricism of my rotting.
Repeat me and grow me.
I wait for you with spengler and gallows from the museum.
Deliver me, I cry, but do not hope.
The slaves no longer believe the beads, generals.
My name is among others napoleon of elba
and st. helena comes later.

(translated by Peter Nijmeijer)

Constant, or Constant Nieuwenhuys, is a Dutch painter who in the late forties and early fifties was a member of the Cobra movement together with other Belgian, Danish, and Dutch artists and writers, among them also Kouwenaar.—Editors' Note.

HAND ETC.

Down the road my hand walks naked on five legs.
He meets another spider.
The spider says I like to live under lace curtains blouses.
And they walk the night falls a womanly woman stands
crying.
The hand consoles her with a dream.

I dreamt I was young.
I rocked in leather waterbags.

It thundered slowly.
I got a gray past full of dust rain.
I threw two black plates on the terrace among the garden
    chairs and sobbing limped through the currant bushes.
I wanted to lie down next to the spider.
But the grafting gardener laughed.
And on five legs I walked to the house of my left father and
    my handy mother and suddenly lived till I woke up.

The womanly woman dries her tears and begins to laugh.
The spider brings out a book and hides the laughing woman
    between the pages.
Reading the hand continues on my way—

                (translated by Peter Nijmeijer)

WITHOUT NAMES

When I see how helplessly the thoughts of many
swarm round the names of things
like caged birds round birdseed
I'd rather climb the nameless thing that is a mountain
if need be halfway

set silence to music
but suppress the name, not out of respect
but rather out of sheer blindness
and so sift accurately
dust fact and time through flesh:
that is an attempt at creation

if need be halfway: the prospect
of a solid thing that releases and leaves out space

highly real is the sleep and the hunger slaked
highly conceivable because unnamed

and the sooner the houses
are gone from hands and eyes
the larger one lives—

(translated by Koos Schuur)

WITHOUT COLORS

Colors—the time will come
that I'll abjure them:
masculine blue, feminine red
childlike yellow
healthy boisterous green
aggrieved purple, creeping pink
deceiving its father and mother
with gentle lies and unrequested
stretching into sulking black
black simply playing the part of night
and white, hairy
illusion of nothing

the time will come
that with pen and colorless ink
I shall lay open mix and immortalize
the man the woman the child
the healthy season and the shoveling grave's edge
the creeping flesh and the mutual
demolition of ravens and mists

as a blind man

as a blind man does not see
what is said to be there
but says what he touches and doubts—

(translated by Koos Schuur)

LIKE AN OBJECT

A poem like an object

a revolving glass door and the chinese waiter
constantly coming back with other dishes

a park attendant filing his nails
amidst siberian children from maine

a prehistoric venus in the company of
a spider on a turnpike

a glass of mother's milk, a starched
tuxedo, yellowed

a bee, a penknife
both stinging, an airplane
dissolving in country rain

a poem like an object—

(translated by Koos Schuur)

FOUND SUBJECTS

The surprise with which one performs
the self-evident over and over again

the bridge that only really exists
when the river is evaporated or frozen

the lover bound to his girl
by a rope of paper

the spaceman declared unfit
because of claustrophobia

the poet who uses his hands
and falls asleep

the words that the next morning
at least reek of the mouth

(translated by Peter Nijmeijer)

WHEN WATER STANDS STILL IT'S STONE

When water stands still it's stone—but
this isn't true: he
who applies language assumes
that for instance the long-drawn gesture
of the ocean frozen on a snapshot
only in passing lacks time, or as
dr burndike (112) remarks in his thesis
caught up with time conclusively
isn't it? isn't it?

it is! but still all these abstractions
don't build up a dike, dike
to bar the water and behind which the villas
raised their roofs sufficiently high

so when the poet says
when water stands still it's stone
he is thinking in generations, but
he is with you alone—

(translated by Peter Nijmeijer)

PLACE: SOMEWHERE

Place: somewhere
action: heat
this is so doesn't happen, one smells
a sardine, a thick one

see also the flies
like flying machines flying
in the heat which is hot
hear also the heated flies

witness the things present
water is scarce is water
slowly stands still in heat
still also the flies present

sing of the exact thickness
of the tinned sardine, know somewhere
in this inside the senses fabricate
and hibernate—

(translated by Peter Nijmeijer)

4 VARIATIONS ON

I
The overmastering of the mud
the flattest use of the eyes

then the sifting through the finest inference
the enlargement on scale

the formation of almost, deformation
of certain, steeling

of water, attempt
at a peephole to the closed

2
Many allay the mother the holy time
or seek to thicken I

spy I spy something you can't
or conjugate the question mark or

cover the wound with the father's mouth
may a lot of breath be their part

but all gnaw at something they make: death
doing to breathe everything

3
What is dead is elsewhere
and nothing, one is a child knows little

of less, drinks light
like milk from a flask

like the sand embezzling the rain
and enjoying it in the dark

with an ice-cream cone vanishing down a dark lane
and then summer is over

4
What's there is the endless clear country road
the immoderately eternal country road

stretching on its way to the resting point
resting on its way to the farthest point

on the grass a mug and a newspaper, so low
to the ground that no one asks where

a minute ago one walked there so black and cocksure
that one fused with one's target

(translated by Peter Nijmeijer)

LANDSCAPE LEFT BEHIND

I
And so your landscape became old, even
what was lucky enough to be inedible
became digested

once you stepped by mistake on a butterfly
and what happened happened, at home
an angel slipped out of your name, your mouth
took over your lips, inkblot
and vetch, over and over again

2
home is the hunter, very old
earth on your body, you stood
in your wall like a window

you looked down on your slow-motion fields, the bed
that made you immortal for a day
made you familiar with death

a poem reciting itself, blinking
from your windowpane as long
as there was light

3
nothing left to write, everything cast-iron, everything
cram-packed with time

and your way slipping away at the end, nothing
should remain

over your landscape the same landscape, hand
in glove, everywhere spaces
where the poem was

(translated by Adrian Henri)

Bert Schierbeek
(1918–   )

I FASTEN DOWN THE DAY

I fasten down the day
the every day
upon the seald field of the seconds
inside the wrapper and bract of the times
the fipple flute lifted up to the image of this reed tongue in
the wounded mouth which the tree is going to build
from a snatchd and contemplating passage of the voice
majestic as a jungle
embracing the unseen water
the fear in the animals' throats
the stride and the stance of the proud flamingo
the wingèd imprint of the hands hewn in stone desert
so as to shift the tonalities generation the crossbeam of
language
the avatar
the dada
the wondertree of this head-manual
living in the windladder of keynotes
the ascending
the descending
the madrigalian flood of the common names
the mystery city of the voice
the sub-and-super thing

my cool man's eye raised up
my throat pilot-and-sun light
the wondrous keel of this ship capsized upon earth
the hull of this scallop is transparent
lacrimaculture the universe of the heart
the ear the circumvamping carcass
the inadequate action of the hands up there
the picture of the disturbd
"I" in my voice
the one who imitates the sound
I lie down at the coast and listen
in the terrifying clench of the presence
a black pope
a knight of light
a fable fountain
of the mudbath of the human voice

(translated by Charles McGeehan)

LOOK A MAN GOES TO KANSAS

look a man goes to Kansas and buys a horse
$550
and asks the dealer: please deliver this horse to me in New
    York
$600
and furthermore: I live at 57th Street, that's where I want it
$610
when the dealer arrives with the horse he says: I want to
    have it up on the thirteenth floor
$620
at the thirteenth floor he says: I want it in the bathroom
$630
then the dealer asks: now you've paid $630 for this horse and
    you put it in the bathroom. Why?

Because all these years I've been living with a friend who
    finds that nothing new ever happens; now at least I can
    say to him: go to the bathroom and he'll see a horse
dealer says: Oh . . . and leaves

(translated by Charles McGeehan)

DEATH, SAID REMCO

death, said Remco
is an emotional stir
now I know better
death is a smack
jamming brakes screeching tires
clattering glass
and lying dead-still
on the street
alone
death is red
and still
    your last word
    still in my ear
    that is dead

death said Remco
is an emotional stir
I cannot steer, rudderless now

at night
and during-the-day
I call you back
and do you then arise
out of the grave?
on which is inscribed
Awaken from the dream

Awaken!—from the dream
which life is
says the inscription

such is life
that I feel ashamed
that I'm yet alive
and am ashamed
and go on living
and sometimes I'm ashamed

(translated by Charles McGeehan)

Remco is Remco Campert.—Editors' Note.

BIRD SINGS

bird sings
branch breaks
bird falls
bird flies
bird sings

(translated by Charles McGeehan)

ISHI

Ishi
the last one of his tribe
a redskin
is cherished
(he remembers all about his tribe
the woods, the animals and plants)

as a hunter
he is unequaled
he is Ishi
the last one
and lives in a museum
(he shapes points for arrows, makes
the shafts and bows, and may not
shoot at the whites with them)
they cherish Ishi
the last one
he works in their museum
(the whites love Ishi)
(the last one)
up to the day he died
of tuberculosis
of which no white
(they love him)
dies anymore
only Ishi
the last one
of his tribe

(translated by Charles McGeehan)

THE SUN: DAY

1) Sun comes up
   whole World's red
   me too

2) Sun climbs—
   red cart, ow—
   over my leg

3) take piece of wood
   in rising Sun
   carve myself new leg

4) I drink in Sun
   dress up leg with shoe
   leg itches too

5) Sun higher, me drunk
   long hours of daytime
   come along

6) tired of leg
   think of windmills
   get sleepy

7) Sun devours color
   leg gets whiter
   black sheep too

8) I in dream
   make mills for Wind
   which rushes up

9) angry woman comes
   takes bottle away
   "windmills" she says

10) what my head thinks
    my hands make
    World trembles

11) Wind lies down
    under roof of fig tree
    Sun and me too

12) weave basket
for Sun and me
sheep sleep

(translated by Charles McGeehan)

THE SUN: NIGHT

1) Sun goes down
whole World's red
me too

2) lie in my garden
leg itches
the wooden one

3) 'm drunk
my head's purple
Sea too

4) angry woman sleeps
me in my basket
with Sun

5) all colors which Sun ate
she gives back
in dream

6) wings of windmills
turn round full-of-color
fig tree stands still

7) my head spins round
like Sun
in his Sea

8) Sea eats me all–day–long
   gives me back
   at night

9) shadow over the Land
   everything black
   sheep too

10) woman comes out of house
    chases sheep away
    fig tree trembles

11) I take up
    basket in Sun
    bird screeches

12) Sun comes up
    whole World's red
    me too

(translated by Charles McGeehan)

Remco Campert
(1929–   )

A PRESIDENT IN HIS COUNTRY RESIDENCE

Mamie and I, we haven't known
A peace like this in thirteen years,
A peace like this in this silent house,
With the fields and plane trees all around
And no main road within fifteen miles.

In fear and earnest for all those years
We worked as duty would have us do
In the white house where the floorboards creaked
With military violence
(The shoes of the coming and departing general).

I don't mean to say that our marriage has now
Entered upon a second spring,
Yet we live much closer to one another
Than ever before and every day
Content is now my portion with Mamie.

It is the tender breath of nature
(Don't I know how a moonlit night
Can nestle here in the garden chairs)
That makes us so peaceful, so relaxed.
Fruit juice in the morning, at noon a verse
By Robert Frost.

I saw wars come and peace depart,
But those one can get through
With humanity
And a steadfast heart. In the evenings I play
Solitaire with Mamie. And then another
Day is done.

(translated by James Brockway)

POETRY IS AN ACT . . .

Poetry is an act
of affirmation. I affirm
I live, I do not live alone.

Poetry is a future, thinking
of next week, of another country,
of you grown old.

Poetry is breath, moving
my feet, sometimes with hesitation,
over the demanding earth.

Voltaire had a pox, but
cured himself by drinking 200 pints
of lemonade amongst other things: and that's poetry.

Or take the surf. Beaten to bits
on the rocks but not beaten,
resumes the assault and thus is poetry.

Each written word
is an onslaught upon old age.
Death wins at last, for sure,

but death is merely the silence in the theater
when the last word is spoken.
Death is an emotion.

(translated by John Scott and Graham Martin)

IMAGINE

Imagine: we were snowed in.
We were running out of food,
Radio was out of order, shoes split,
We stoked the fire with notebooks
Filled with memories to gain bleak heat

And the flag, that we ought to have
Planted somewhere, we used
For a blanket of course. There was
Absolutely no hope left at all,
Not even hope for hope. Yet

I was not unhappy, because
Death went hand in hand with
So many declarations of love
From you to me, me to you,
That I never got around to

Unhappy feelings. There
Was no time. There would always be
Breasts to kiss, eyes
To reveal and the times we were tired
We fell asleep and dreamed about

President Roosevelt.

(translated by Greta Kilburn)

SPARROWS

I,
no, it was Caligula, fat,
half-bald and 29
(you remember that winter),
died
a dishonorable, prosaic death
in the darkened entrance to a theater
at the whispering hands of an assassin.

Caligula (jackboots, once
jovial, prodigal, human),
not in the claws of a beast,
but between the thighs of his sister
"which seemed to him an excellent Egyptian custom,"
but no luster
in the darkened entrance to a theater.

But what am I talking about? About
the bygone gristle
of someone who, it turned out, was a sparrow,
thin skull, no god, no golden rain,
naked as men,
as sparrows, as sparrows
and men. Done to dust
at the shabby hands of the ludicrous world.

(translated by John Scott and Graham Martin)

THIS HAPPENED EVERYWHERE

This happened everywhere:
the unemployed loiterers,
the war-wounded dreaming
of a street full of co-ops,
the restless pensioners
to whom a great wrong was done.

Damps of the night
still hung about the city—
tired and shivering I left the café,
morning greeted the mountains.

A blind man sold lottery tickets
to stray dogs and lame alcoholics
and in front of an embassy
a sturdy wench scrubbed the step.
But for whoever's not in bed with a whore or his wife
the city mornings are asexual.

And the absurd posters
for the bullfight the football match
the hundredth performance—
letters letters letters,
the circus has long since left.

I went further
into the healthy countryside
over chalk-white roads,
whilst the thirsty sun drank me dry—
or took the tram,
my ticket wet with the first rain,
back to my unfurnished room,
the unpaid rent and oblivious sleep.

(translated by John Scott and Graham Martin)

WOULD YOU BELIEVE IT?

Would you believe it?
I was just a young lad
scribbling verses about
the birch tree's silver stem

whilst all around me
the huge drunkenness
of the Liberation:
water had turned into whiskey.

Everything boozed up and screwed,
Europe one great mattress
and the heavens the ceiling
of a third-rate hotel.

And me, timid youth,
obliged to sing
the pure birch bark
its delicate shy leaves.

(translated by John Scott and Graham Martin)

HURRAH, HURRAH

There are seas, there are mountains
hurrah.
There are pinball machines with fantastic flippers
and with very slack ones.
Hurrah, hurrah.
This is the S. of F. in winter,
letter from Menton.

Dear Gerrit, it's lousy with old people here
hurrah.

They drive about in terribly expensive cars
skip along the sea
perform tricks for their dogs
take out their dentures and cackle with them
wear gas masks from the 14/18 war
against the winter sun
and the sea wind which sometimes tugs at their leather caps
and carries them away, hurrah.
They're having a ball in the hour of death,
am I to hold my own?
I'll be dying anyway

but why should I hurry?

There are seas, there are mountains
with fantastic pinball flippers—
I flip and I flip and I flip.
And though that's no consolation
it's a fact nonetheless
hurrah
as I too will weigh a limited number of ounces one day
hurrah, hurrah
in a vase or (more likely) a rotting box
hurrah.

There are hard new buildings
and they'll collapse too I guess
hurrah
but this doesn't alter the fact:
didn't I back a winner today?
clean-shave my jawbones?
eat meat?
don't I smoke my fill
and doesn't radio monte-carlo non-stop broadcast
jolly programs?

(translated by Greta Kilburn)

Gerrit is Gerrit Kouwenaar.—Editors' Note.

CITY PARK

We often come to the City Park
and so do the Jews of Antwerp

Families in their Sunday best
the air is full of Yiddish

my daughter dutifully spoons strawberry yoghurt
I drink coffee or Stella beer

read the paper
in the Milk Bar of the City Park

where it's nice and green
and will get nicer and brown

for autumn approaches
(buy your tickets now for the coming season)

in the pond lies a white boat
(City of Antwerp) going to rot

the trees have all got names
which I'm forgetting again

and by the bandstand men sit playing cards
in the evening they're still sitting

by the fierce light of a lamp
(in the bushes behind Dr. Caligari skulks about)

on the lawn a Moroccan lies sleeping
sandals on feet, newspaper over face

for ten francs you can hire a deckchair all day
baby-sitters earn twenty francs an hour

and further up amongst the trees run little boys
with long sideburns and dark blue skullcaps

the adolescent girls have runs in their stockings
and they let themselves be kicked by lanky youths

my daughter is fair and will become a filmstar
but I'm still reading her Donald Duck aloud

the ducks in the ponds wear no jackets
and nothing much happens to them in the City Park

where the trueborn citizens of Antwerp no long come
or so I'm told by a writer

modern
progressive

and when I ask him why not he says:
because there are so many Jews there

and goes on talking about
literature

(translated by John Scott and Graham Martin)

LETTERS

I should write him and him
that I'm in good health
that I was drunk last night in a Greek café
after that in a Turkish café, a Norwegian café

that I am preparing myself
for an extravagantly high gas bill

and other things to others—
browsing in an ever more inexplicable world

that someone said:
you Dutchmen, you're all the same
even though I had picked up the check
and was wearing a French pair of glasses
and what's more had a book of German poems in my pocket
and at home on the table
Anne Sexton's inimitable poem
"wanting to die"

and listen how I put in new fuses
and suddenly the light went on again
and she was lying asleep on the couch
beneath the blue blanket

I should write to this one and that one
that I won't do it
that I refuse
that I'm taking it to court
that the days here wear away in rain
and the world is never larger than a town
than me in that town
my feet on those cobblestones
and what I see when I blink my eyes
and I should ask how things are
whether the house is built
the play well translated
if the children are thriving
and the wives not all too unhappy

(translated by James S Holmes)

1975

Strange years, these years,
nothing to laugh about, a lot that's flopped
rolling stones with no moss.

Poetry limps back home
the warm lamp
the petty pain of calling daddy-mamma
sadness at the birthday past
nature again a consolation
that wretched God rearing his head again
disguised now as a neo-Calvinist student
or a Catholic Marxist nitwit.

But we too
when we made a bid for greatness
had nothing to offer anyone
that provided shelter
food in the belly
shears to cut the barbed wire
hardly even a rag to staunch the bleeding
or beauty to burn a poem.

Run wild on snowswept plains
deserts caught inside walls
the cellars camps and cages
where one man turns wolf to another.

All those dreams all those years
over and over that child at the burnt-down station
the high shriek in the barracks
where the lovely vase of your voice
was shattered.

And outside the gates
the cold cameraman
always worried about his equipment.

Writing a silly extravagance
where even breathing was luxury
and eating, your plate empty.

The finest talents hooked on drink
on fame, on vanity
on the needle
or in the asylum,
with a place on a committee
or jumped out a window
or huddling at home with the little woman
or getting lost in analyses:
napalm of words
on the skin of language.

Oh
beat us about the ears
till we come awake
till our emotions are
no longer lost in meek bleats
till we take up our beds again
and go a-roving with the beggar boy
the beggar maid

(translated by James S Holmes)

TUFT BY TUFT

The grass comes up tuft by tuft
there where last year fire bared ground

in awkward cooperation
body and the brain contained in it
push on paper a blade of a word

gasping for air

along

immediately behaving
as if it had always been there

(translated by James S Holmes)

Sybren Polet
(1924–   )

SHADOW

A house with antipodes

A house with eyelids. I push
my recalcitrant shadow
ahead of me,
to smolder in the sun,
dissolve in a stone.

—there's a weak contact in stone—

I carry my shadow in a box
like a dead organ
in search of a skeleton.

In my pocket I carry
an ivory monkey of shadow
to fumble.

I put a small fleshy shadow
on the table
and puff and puff—fluorescent
an image approaches:

a counter-man.

(translated by James S Holmes)

CELEBRATION

He knows it, he has a
foreboding: tomorrow he

will be born, and now there's already
merriment one day too soon; I was born

just one day too soon. I shoot a flag;
a blue one this time, not a white one but a

blue one, I form my own sky.
May it be permitted. At the latest tomorrow,

together with the one best loved,

together with 311 eyewhite gulls
and an ethereal wasp for a sun,

at the top of my voice I wrestle him into
his new world in my banner of skin.—O,

he knows it, he has a foreboding,
he is a small rude wonder

of once per moon, once per grace per
moon; and now he already plays Adam, rustling

with inspiration. He's an orchestra, in me
an orchestra, walks

in front of the orchestra, walks even
faster than the trees walk and

away—; well, it's
fun by me, it's OK by

me. I'm happy to leave myself behind,
among the trees, a tree, inside me

there's nothing to expect; I roll in the sun.
I don't leave a single projection behind.

Don't leave even a religious projection behind.

(translated by James S Holmes)

RE-EDUCATION

I put my father in his cradle,
tucked him in, gave him his bath, his pacifier.
He grew, like a tree of flesh, faster than I,
sucking himself full of the past.
He slept my sleep, dreamed his unruly dreams
in me, engulfed me with his humanity.

I rocked him as one rocks his dearest ancestor,
kissed his small bald head, hummed
folk tunes that sounded like modern music,
but the younger he was/became, the more
he became my future, faster each time I woke again
than I could grow or wake.

I made him go to school, punished him
for his frivolous faith in God, his conjugal fidelity
that prevented all rebirth or stamped me premature;
I smacked him for his exemplary goodness,
almost begging him to be wrong, begging for his old
all too temporal eternity.

He grew to be a man (like me), ate (like me),
got married (like me) and caused conclusively the birth of

kicking and unwilling me: let him be punished;
let him be punished with a perfect happiness
in a before-life suited to his personality: father
of four believers: his lot: a garden full of heavenly

toys, a boy's bicycle, four cigarettes of health
for each day off, a third (glass) eye for magnifying purposes,
a bit of extra eroticism for the weekend and finally
an everlasting pension for the future and

Let him be punished who shall ever harm this man.

(translated by André Lefevere)

THE HUMAN USE OF HUMAN BEINGS

With my muscles running out into a radio,
                        with my muscles,
in the headlights of a nightly motorcar,
                        with my muscles,—
with my nerves reacting in a telex machine,
in the soft green eye of an ailing homunculus,
                        with my nerves,—
with my words born or delivered in exile,
spontaneous or by caesarian section,
                        with my words, words . . .

The words of tomorrow are outdated today,
impromptu poets perish in their own words: elec-
tricians, prematurely appointed, precociously warm
with dying . . . I have seen a man . . .

I have seen a man, larger
than all my thoughts piled up in cold storage;

long he was, like a continent, like an ocean
deep in the immensity of his economy,
immeasurable too
was his body population, unfathomed
the heat of his intestines. I have seen that man.

I have seen that man, I was inside him, I had to word him.
I was his intestines, his thief, his electrician,
his word my word no word, his word has passed away.

The True-Man sparks no more. The True-Man
thinks no more.
Mr. True-Man became human
                              and lived amongst us.

                              (translated by Peter Nijmeijer)

TOMORROW'S IDEAS

tomorrow's ideas /
                    are today's realities, date
becomes fate / and vice versa. Self-service philosophy.)
Someone, Unperson for instance, has the time wrong.
Tobaccobirds flutter. And see, it's as if I walk again
in the future, hand in hand with an afterfather, the way I
    used to.
His heredity descends on me like a dove.
Between projections, big as elephants, 190-year-old
adolescents—the air full of alien intelligences—
we saunter todaywards.——I am amazed (:: Mr X!)
Does he really exist, I ask, like me? / Smiling: like *you?*—
The hole in history closed / open / closed:
amiably blinking spectacles that—
                              8 months. Thumbpainting

with edible fingerpaint—orange / green / red—
a stripe, a scratch, a smudge—*"Like real!"*—natively cre-
    ative—
"A real Mondrian!"—a speck, a stripe, a curl—purr, purr—
natively creative—pink and prinked—eating the speck the
    stripe
the Mondrian—mm—*"Perfect art consumption"*—Later: the
    mouth
and foot paintings of invalids. (He buys the reproductions
reluctantly.)
        Then: still later and better, because not himself
    but seen
on TV: a neurosis-less testtube baby—grown on uterine
sponge tissue—sweet tadpole with gills, the umbilical
cord in the void, or else, contented carbaby, greedily
gulping carbon monoxide and cooing like a transistor radio—
"I wish I was a pair of twins /
                then I'd go play together."
O cauliflower baby, nostril baby, anus baby, forehead baby—

                (translated by James S Holmes)

ALIENATION & ALLITERATION

He :: She. / Here :: There. /
                X :: X-ess.
The (their) smile goes
              from hand to hand.
Vaults itself to a coin.
              Fingers exchange
in a friendly duel of hands. / Act
                like never before.

They say: Also per telecommunication
   their relationship's OK and
   their indirect financial contact
gives rise to content: erotics
at arm's length.

                :: Objectified love
—round or square—is likewise
their furniture, their fauna.
                    Their flora
won't die, will never die, for it needs
   no water no lemonade.

Through the unnaturally clear
                        windowpane
—blue— : panoramic art. Right.
   Ever-green grass. Right.
   No sun- or moonset
smolders or discolors
               the colors of nature.

A magnetic goat
          is grazing on the lawn,
bleatless. A clockwork dog
   stands guard at the door,
barkless.

          —Silence. Hush . . .
                    It is
almost
     a hereafter
          on *this* earth:

                (translated by Peter Nijmeijer)

Jan G. Elburg
(1919–   )

YOUNG OLD YOUNG OLD

When I am old
the brazen sun god will strike
his barb down on me

the old man has stories
the young man confidence
and I the shrill song

they rolled a child's drum
filled with water
the feet cocked their toes
asked the snails the beat
each walked his own way

when I am young
"use your own wings
don't hope for
the angling clouds"

they tootled on a trumpet
full of hay and dung
the legs did their best
to follow

when I am old
when I am young
o that I have to reeve my leaves
and on the way
leave my wings behind.

(translated by Koos Schuur)

SATIE

Like that again:
livorno hanneshagen
the room throws long pears
(at the)

windows snicker openly
when the sedate housekeeper
moves her breast fins
(in a twilight of black thread)

in a twilight of black thread
madness sits like a gallant
lorelei high on the cupboard
(and dreams)

this is so far from dreaming
that a small head would rather come
out of the wall
(to)

as a consolation for this man alone
—he is smoking something like a white bone—
who careens around here in a sketched car

his beard of living flies
frames the mirror.

(translated by André Lefevere)

THE AXES RUST

Grown up under the sun
grown crooked under the caresses
of jealous winds
man imitates a tree
and stands, gnarled and sturdy,
in a wild field

each alone in his own chaotic swamp:
the women with a mask of blossom,
the men with a barely fluttering
flag of crenated leaves,
and soon in the same way the children
the now still sweet-smelling shrubs.

grown up under the clouds,
alone at war with the stars.

no bird still whets its voice
against the timber of their shoulders;
never a bumblebee takes droning
out of their ears
the lasting melody
of wind and far-off thunder.

while they grow up crooked and sturdy
an incessant listening to
the gulping water and their own rustling
is their occupation,

that and standing gnarled, no nation,
no forest, neither here
nor on the heights near the horizon.

under the sagging roofs of the barns
the axes rust.
there is no footfall and no beat of wings.

(translated by Koos Schuur)

KNOWLEDGE OF WHAT IS

Landscape of loneliness
invisible as coins on dead eyes
but perceivable:
over a sloping field of backlighted fumes
the roads lead into one rigid wave.
the body a sleeping manifesto
like the bird folded up in a log.

a fingertip of silence stirs the eardrums
as cold lips instruct the mouth that without sound
sums up the experienced:

the stone-bespattered
infinite sea of nothingness
stands in the flesh.
more void than so-called life
is man.

vista of the lonely
taste of the inhospitable
as snow against the palate.
I.

(translated by Koos Schuur)

SOMETIMES BELIEVING

Praise the day before night falls
before your golden fiancée breaks it off
before the dark cover makes it dark

praise the day and tell before night falls
how it was what there was that it was good
tell it to ears still half-believing

praise the day praise the mess
of whirring tin the noise and the fear
praise the wind for the leaking garbage bag
praise the light on the shit the leer of the ugly
woman and the lick of the hairless dog praise
the smell of hot asphalt, sweat and french fries

praise the godwholly godforgotten
good lubberly irreplaceable life
before you exit driveling stumbling shouted down and out

praise it
while the long night draws nearer
while the thumb emphatically moves towards your throat.

(translated by André Lefevere)

Paul Rodenko
(1920–1976)

FEBRUARY SUN

Again the world goes open like a girl's room
from white remotenesses street scenes come sailing up
workers with alum hands are building
a windowless house of stairways and pianos.
The poplars with a schoolboy inclination
toss each other a ball full of bird voices
and way up high an invisible airplane
paints bright blue flowers on bright blue silk.

The sun plays at my feet like a serious child.
I wear the downy mask of
the first spring breeze.

(translated by James S Holmes)

ROBOT POETRY

Poetry, cruel machine
Voice without voice, tree
Without shadow: gigantic

Beetle, scorpion poetry
Armored robot of language—

Teach us with planing words
To peel the rampant flesh from the bones
Teach us with pincering words
To squeeze off the fingers of bleating emotion
Teach us with taut rustling words
To break through the manyvoiced barrier of the soul:
Teach us to live in the deadly vacuum
The pure and faceless pain, the poem

(translated by James S Holmes)

HE

He is an eagle's head smaller than I
And has only five fingers to each hand
He thinks he is me
He says he is I
He sways in my shoulders
Like an infant moon in an ancient river

He sways, he weighs, I can't shake him off
He lives in my shadow, he lies in my truth
He lives on my shredding shadow as
A clock on the stench of illness, I can't
Shake him off, the robot, the false
Prophet, I can't shake him off
He leers through two of my eyes
He runs on the warmth of my body
He builds like an ant in my darkness
He calls himself lord of my light
He calls himself I

The dawn-lifting beat of my wings, the wheel
Of my white-hot winging-out he dreams
Into faraway tales of blood and horses
My one almighty word he crumbles
To ten thousand greedy and lipless mouths
Which shriek for bread between him and the world
Which stand like a tent between him and the world
Which he calls: world
Seated on his throne as a meek king
A soapstone fetish
A bard

He sways in my shoulders
He rows in my breath
He thumps in my belly
I can't shake him off

He folds his hands in my ocean
He jubilates: an urn, a god, a palace
When I take off his god like a glove
He says: science is a house
And time is matter, he always knows better
He is man, the all-eater
With a head like an angry young moon
He knows what he knows
And calls himself I

He calls himself I
He sways in my shoulders
He thumps in my belly
Someday I'll bear him
A mangod of ashes
Ha!

(translated by Ramón E. du Pré)

Jan Hanlo
(1912–1969)

TO ARCHANGEL

I was walking in the park in spring
And it smelled of camels
True there were lots of people
But still it probably came from
The water in the ponds
Camels
I can't
Abide
Your scent
With camel's hair I'll go fishing
Amongst the lotuses and rushes
Without fishing
Pole or fishhook
With my angel
In Archangel
My angel smells of
Ears of wheat
Newfallen snow
And leaves

(translated by James S Holmes)

ONE MORNING

For Mai

Half past four one April morning
I was walking and whistling the St. Louis Blues
But I whistled it my way
And whistling I thought: may my whistling
be like the song of the great thrush
And what do you know, after a while my
whistling of the St. Louis Blues
really *was* like the song of the great thrush:
turdus viscivorus

(translated by James S Holmes)

THE ROOF

for R. and F.

They stood looking four stories high on the roof
I said they should go or else they'd fall off
A boy and a girl I didn't know them
In a city the houses are extra high
: If you fall off you're sure to be dead
They obliged me and went away
But when I looked out of my window a little later
The boy was standing at the very edge of the roof
He stared abstractedly down past his shoes
Between the toes of his shoes down into the depths
The thought of death didn't startle him
I spoke very sternly Boy get away from the edge
I'll go tell your father and mother
He went. Or aren't they home? He shook his head

They weren't home. Later I heard their seesaw in the attic
They seesawed together long and happily
And sang glad songs while they did it

(translated by James S Holmes)

VERSE AS OF 7 JUNE 1951

You mean Josje with the tiny eyes?
No, with the big eyes.
You mean Josje with the shrill voice?
No, with the pretty voice.
You mean Josje with the hair that smells of nothing?
No, with hair that smells nice.
You mean Josje that you never think about?
No, that I always think about.
You mean Josje who doesn't like to note down English
    words?
No, who does like to.
But who writes with written letters?
No, who writes with big printed letters.
But who always writes the words in a sentence separately?
No, who writes a lot of the words in a sentence run to-
    gether.
You mean Josje who's saving for a boat?
No, who's saving for a flashlight.
You mean Josje who doesn't like you at all?
No, I mean Josje who likes to be with me.

(translated by James S Holmes)

Hans Warren
(1921–   )

A MOORISH FRIGATE: 2

Waiting for the gazelles
by the ilex tree at the window.
Wind withdrew through every gate
in the palace of memory.
My summer is a Moorish frigate
in full red sail
that hopes to run aground on a reef of pirates.

I love you, I am unworthy;
wind; purify me—
I hurt above the eyes of the night.
Rustling wind in the open window of awareness,
rising wind behind my tough shins,
summer wind,
deliver me to the powdered caliphate of dreams,
the cramp in my nostrils
grows cold to my very heart.

Lo, the boy in the ballet
of the soft, buzzing cobwebs,
the boy with the full, hard calves,
the devil's eyes kohled black,
the broad chest and much too red mouth;

he has a heart like a broken bottle,
a rattling missile of pain, and feet
like panthers slinking towards their prey;
he plays professionally with women
like a bored girl with her dolls
and writes the arabesque of life in gestures
his alchemy transmutes pain to desire
his tears are violoncellos of delight,
his dead are gods rubbed with oil;
his distant love emerges from his blood's mirror.

O lazy summer of the heavy grain spikes
I have not forgotten how to complain with pathos
like a swan beneath a weeping willow:
I am the weatherglass of silence,
my eyes the warm
convulsive mirrors of your tale.
The wine glows like a comma in my stomach,
feel my hands: hot seismographs
of what the dream-herb rouses in me.

The pores of night are wide open,
a green sea lion lies sleeping mildly
a dragon in its red-gilt suit of scales
glides into the park, and cautiously
you place the downy ashes of my poems
in porcelain urns on the window sill.
You say, "The young grain
waves unabsorbed in my memory,
songbirds lie blown together like dry leaves
beneath the age-old oaks of my youth.
I love the wind like a plowman dressed in blue."

Then the gazelles run from your arms
into my open veins.

(translated by James S Holmes)

A SOAP BUBBLE: 3

You knew what you did when you laughed,
you were intrigued, and handsome,
you could hardly know how handsome
for someone as Greek as I am.

And you with that strange grace
of full twenty-five and yet
a dark ephebe, with wise eyes
run away from Patmos.

We didn't need any words
to find out what the score was.
You bowed like a slave, I nodded, the master,
that was the only difference now.

Then after a very teasing wink
we were back in the antique world
of equality—only
as our lips threatened to meet each other
did twenty-four centuries fall away
and a shadow of sadness glide nearer.

(translated by James S Holmes)

THE AGING POET

Last night—I couldn't sleep
even though it finally cooled off—
I went to the sleazy café.
It had almost wound down into silence.
Men hung on their chairs half asleep;
a skinny, dark-skinned kid

looked up in hope, his hand
almost unconsciously rubbing
over his rancid fly.
In a corner, with eyes like light bulbs
sat the aging poet. How often
I'd wished that. "Is your love
on the cruise," he asked. I nodded.
"I'm Suleiman," whispered the boy;
"I'll do everything you want, everything."
"I knew him when I was a kid
myself," said the gray-haired poet;
"when he lay naked in my bed
it was as if I looked in the mirror."

Suleiman's hair smelled of wood fires,
his body bitter, and the famous poet
watched approvingly in the mirror
all night long.

(translated by James S Holmes)

Hans Andreus
(1926–1977)

COUNTRYSIDE IN FRANCE

The houses pick like hens into the landscape,
freckled with poor woods and slanting brown fields.
A church stands like a nine-year-old and curly child;
blue careless smoke drifts somewhere slowly upwards;
sun and moon shiver white and pale-white in the same gray
    sky.

I want to play on the telegraph lines;
I want to turn loose sea horses:
they are so earnest and so beautiful, and never aware that one
    smiles;
I'm as far away as the word Dodecanese.

I'm as afraid as the last leaf on a tree in winter:
it has grown so thin that one sees only its veins;
it has lost its faith in birds.

I remember:

I rounded your breasts,
prolonged your thighs, bound your feet Japanese,
smoothed your shoulders, lighted your eyes
and sang your mouth to you.

But I'm no longer here; I am
farther away than earth and skies.

(written in English)

MULISH

If you knew how mulish, reluctant,
my love for you is,
even though I love you
with my body's assurance
and with an angry trust
in the divine imp on my shoulder.

And if you knew how shyly
I gaze at this: us two in a room,
dovetailing into each other—
and no single word of sense
rising to its feet,
like the evening's witty speaker.

And if you knew
how daft and drunk I go towards the future,
believing—since believe I must—
in this, our composite sign:
youwomaniman, and thinking:
Time took up his pen and wrote it.

(translated by James Brockway)

HORROR STORY

It was one strange and rainy
spring when he had to
take up with death again:
an encounter on the edge of the funnel,
a fistfight around the mouth of nothing.

And that same spooky spring
it came to pass that the woman
he wanted to tilt to his god the sun
and loved like the earth, gnarled spices,
earth with the hand of the sun on its heart,

came to pass that she lifted her eyes
to a soft pair of witch-thin lips twisting softly
round a never completely successful smile—
and slowly slowly snowed in beneath
an eiderdown of lies.

(Crows and blackbirds
flying in circles
cawed endearingly,
spat at the sun,
spat at the earth.)

That was one rainy spring,
one weeping summer and one fall as clear
as a bell of light that's finally sounded.
But in vain. For the crows and blackbirds cawed
and now it's winter.

(translated by James S Holmes)

WORDS FOR YOU

Take hold of them,
these words that come
to caress you now.

Small grain sheaf
walks.

Flaxen damsel
sleeps.

O a red
pimpernel
on a dune crest.

O a red
pimpernel
on a dune crest.

That's number two.

Yes o yes you my
bit of seabreeze
across a white
northerly atoll.

Yes o yes my
lightly falling
deftly nestling
seabird's breastfeather.

O petit pit that peers—
and then broader seen by me:
O dancer's belly of a
belly dancer.

Small warm nest
of sudden yet
darkening grass:

O my pit of love.

Into which I fall.

(translated by James S Holmes)

I SPOKE THE WORDS OF THE WORLD

I spoke the words of the world
round earth words
sunwords and moonwords
the words the animals spoke

I studied palmistry
and I learned astrology
and gold from stones my alchemy
inverted dreams my artistry

I made statues out of marble
and I kindled a red fire
I breathed my music
lining finely oiled paper

Nothing nothing was enough
words breaking like waves
on your archaic smile and your eyes
deep inside the earth deep inside

But it was all I had
beyond my skin beyond my hands
beyond my blinded lips
beyond my muted eyes

And I ask you now to listen
as you stand still and listen to birds
as you stand still and see the sun
as you caress my body in your arms

I know you are somewhere
in the mystery word
in the translated word
in the word the wonder of the world

I spoke the words of the world
round earth words
sunwords and moonwords
the words the animals spoke

(translated by Johanna H. Prins)

THE EMPTY ROOM IS STILL AN EMPTY ROOM

The empty room is still an empty room,
only myself in it and no one opening
the door, no woman or friend, no stranger.
I have been here before but now
I am many years older,
many more, and it is more difficult to know
that this will pass, that I will
walk free from this sick man, maybe,
but still
in the light which I have loved.

(translated by Johanna H. Prins)

HOLLOW OF LIGHT

Talking to emptiness.

Hollow of light.

Essence that hides
and keeps on hiding
the radiant lack
of form and circumference

for eyes that want to
see and can't.

But I talk to it
with my mouth and hands,
my entire body

until it speaks,
answers and
breaks free.

(translated by James S Holmes)

Cees Nooteboom
(1933–   )

A THOUSAND NIGHTS AND DAYS

Like a king on a surly island
the wind scours the evening up and down.
I hunt for my invisible life.
The wings of my eyes burn.

The birds turn blacker;
A copper evening resounds in the mountains.
Under the trees in the wood peace grazes,
but no one believes it.

All the bushes hide soldiers.
The grit of the rain licks at the water.
The copper runs stale and crumbles.
Only I fly about with my humiliated unrest.

Never once shall I meet my own body:
A guilty curtain separates me forever from myself.

(translated by Peter Nijmeijer)

THE SLEEPING GODS

Reticent as the mouths of shells,
among praying dogs and the irreverent whistling of light,
made wild and useless by their solitude,
the glossy gods decay in their gilded beds.

Outside, their obsolete horses are waiting.
The jewels have been stolen from their chariots.
Empty remain the saddles, empty the chariots,
decayed and covered by the mould of space.

Alone under the black of night
the faithful creep to the walls of the house
and warm themselves on their masters' immortality.

But the white teeth of morning
find everything, sacrifices and horses.
The square of the world is empty, empty is space,
the gods asleep for thousands and thousands of years,
dreaming of the merciful salt of death.

(translated by Peter Nijmeijer)

FEAR MAKES THE SPECTATOR

Desirous, in the lighted sound of his dream,
he bends above the sea, drowns,
and sees the hunting horses
spotted with the love he did not feel.

The golden egg lies in the cracked sun.
His wooden, painted hand reaches out
but it gives way.
Darker now, the child in it curls up.

Dunes or hills, mountains to lie in.
In the levels of his imagination, his shell-like reality,
his soul totters and falters helplessly,
and watches itself burn.

It is love that is burning.
Fear makes the spectator. In a later act
His silver edges have curled up, his eyes have melted.

What remains is time, transformation,
time all the more open and torturing,
empty and debased, made vicious by words.
All that's lacking is everywhere guiltily present.

O Lord who is it there spreads out the tents of heaven.

(translated by Peter Nijmeijer)

FUJI

1

Here, on the dormant, serrated sides,
the wooded, red-brown so snow-white slope,
with fine traces of priests and poets,
radiant or obscure in the world that surrounds
it drifts or sails above spinning mists
a shape without weight,
a mountain of light.

2

Here, armored with walls of ice, seen
through a child's eye among lucid blossoms,
in the black pocket of night, in the mirroring water,
from the dancing deck of a ship, against windows of cars and
      trains,

it stands on the lookout among airstreams and clouds invisi-
ble, visible
roams past through the skies like a migrating bird
or settles on land like a state.

3

"Here," the traveler can say a thousand times to that flowing
dream scene,
"here," paints the painter, drowning in his double landscape,
"here," whispers the fisherman patient on his footbridge of
bamboo, "here,"
"here," and they always seeing something else
and with high butterfly sounds of oo and ee
their lips form the name of the mountain that runs the house
there
appearing and disappearing like a sun or a moon.

4

There, in Yamanaka etched like a fire under water,
under the silken rains of Baiu, in the hive of the summer,
weathered like a statue resting with its feet in the sea
it blows to the clouds and storms on the flute of its craters.
There, with the highest eye on its tower
it is the first to see goraiko, the purple airhole of morning,
the departure of the journeying sun, the high swirl of the
heavens.
All Japan hangs from it, a dream-laden basket
which it lifts and carries through the air
out beyond the region of time.

(translated by Scott Rollins)

TITICACA

I heard the sound of His Name sung
Through the madness and mist of morning.
Against the glowing awning of the East
In a maze of water a mosque
Stood plaited from reeds.
Iraq. Hewn like eyeless statues
The boys stroked the oars.
We glided through the swamps.
Spirits of silence and wood.

On the other cheek of the world
I see stone in the shapes of people
To crush a man to death.
Cruel and full of hatred the world
Always dreams a new thought,
A dagger in waiting water.
In his boat of woven stalks
The silent rower approaches.
His pigs devour the mud,
His wife cuts the reed.

I am the one who must see all
Tribeless coming from nowhere
To the swamp near the Tigris
To the bite of the Andes
Like a rabbit ready for the hunt.

(translated by Scott Rollins)

Hugo Claus
(1929–   )

BEHIND BARS

Saturday Sunday Monday slow week and weak days

A still life a landscape a portrait

A woman's eyelids
Closing as I come near

The landscape with blond cattle wading
With the season of pity
Burnt into the Prussian blue of the fields

So I painted yet another still life
With unrecognizable eyebrows and a mouth like a moon
With a spiral like a redeeming trumpet
In the Jerusalem of my room.

(translated by Theo Hermans)

FAMILY

Father was eating partridge and Mother wasn't there
and I and George talked about murders
and running away and what trains to take
when the sun came rolling into our attic
and lay there shining in the hay
Father cussed and said: God sees me
George ran away
and I went on playing with the trains
moving electrically across the floor
between poles.

(translated by James S Holmes)

MARSYAS

The fever of my song, the vin du pays of my voice
Left him shrinking behind, Wolf's-throat Apollo,
The god who throttled his boys and sang
Fungi, dull knives, wolf's-throat gravelly song.

Then he churled up, despised,
And broke my throat.
I was tied to a tree, I was flayed and nailed up
Until the water of his long-lipped words flowed into my ears
That violently gave way.

Look at me, bound to the ropes of a soundless space,
Flayed and glued to a copper scent,
Pointed,
Aimed,
Pinned like a moth
In a flame of hunger, a swamp of pain.

The nails of the wind reach into my entrails.
The needles of sleet and sand ride in my skin.
No one has ever cured me.
My song hangs deaf-and-dumb on the hedges.
The teeth of my voice reach only to the virgins,
And who is still a virgin or a virgin bridegroom
In these breakers?

(My famined lips emit
Red coral in flakes.
I curse
The chaff and the clover the mob that hangs out
The paternal flag on my roofs—but you are of stone.
I sing—but you are of feathers and stand
Like a bittern, a signpost of mourning.

Or are you a buzzard—there—a cradling buzzard?
Or in the south, lower, a star, the golden Taurus?)

No one has ever cured me.
In my cellars the ore of knowledge is broken open.

(translated by James S Holmes)

THE MOTHER

I am not, I am not but in your earth.
You screamed, your skin quivered
And my bones caught fire.

(My mother, caught in her skin,
Changes with the returning year.

Her eye is light, escapes the passion
Of the years by looking at me
And calling me "the happy son."

She was no stony bed, no animal fever,
Her joints were young cats,

But my skin does not forgive her,
The crickets in my voice are still.

"You have outgrown me," she says,
Slowly washing my father's feet, and falls silent
Like a woman without a mouth.)

When your skin screamed my bones caught fire.
You laid me down, I can never rebear this image,
I was the invited but the slaying guest.

Now, later, I'm a strange man to you.
You see me coming, you think: "He is
The summer, he makes my flesh and keeps
The dogs in me awake."

While you stand dying every day, not together
With me, I am not, I am not but in your earth.
In me your life rots, turning; you do not
Return to me, and I will not recover from you.

(translated by James S Holmes)

THE TOLLUND MAN

Like a kinsman
who rarely appears among his relatives
and is suddenly found sitting in a corner of the room,
a grim king full of silence and discord,
he does not sleep but rests in silence.

No worm has fed on him,
we are the vermin now
with our eager eyes.

In his age of gods and songs,
of wars and ships and
retaliation,
he was strangled with a leather rope
and dumped into his property: the soil, into
an age of ice and iron.

Traces of linseed, of bannock and knotwort
in the intestinal canal:
it was winter when he died, gasping for air
and locked in the clay of the limeless bog.

The village people stood by,
pushed a fork against his throat and nodded
as he was sacrificed to the summer fruits.
Or was he a murderer? A heretic? A deserter?

Kneeling in the vacuum,
his body groped for its property the soil and found neither
       branch nor tree;
revenge did not enter his mind,
for he smiles in the swamp that preserves him.

A chest will rot, bricks pulverize, grass turns to hay and
       mire;
but he lies, man's next of kin for centuries,
caught in the rope, one ear crushed, toothless.

   ("When I in my power mounted you,
   the world seemed magnificent

   until I glowed with spite
   over the withering of things.

   You screamed like hind and dog and sheep
   when I begot your son.

I was a dagger of limewood
in your skin, that infinite morass.")

The acid that preserved him
grows in the grass.
Bowed, he awaits the justice
of what he was.

If there is blood: clotted.
If there is human life: affected by
the tremendous timeless gas and the fingerprints of years.
If there is blue: wiped out
like the blue of your eyes, years later.

("It is a man of clay
who speaks to you.
I have killed and was killed.
The birds are setting in the West.")

In ammonia and dung,
in black spines,
under a hood of lead:
my death.

Am I guilty of rape?
Did I shun the battle?

My mother foresaw all this
when she brought me into this world
of berries, vipers, and lilacs,
in this trap and the swampy mists
of her life.

I never saw it.
Hence this smile,
as I sink deeper into the polder,
like horned cattle with bellows ache.

The children may well be right in shouting
that I look ridiculous because mildewed.

They know what justice is,
though they do not yearn for it.

My hanging is over, though the skin of my neck
will shrink for centuries to come
and you are vexed, down to your very joists,
by what they did to me.

My tongue is sticking out, I no longer speak,
chained henceforth in your clothes
and neighing in your smile
with my blood and my snot and my seed.

If I am such
then so are you.

Groping for some gesture you find yourself
caught in my clamor and disfigured for days on end.

How old are you now?

Will fire be your punishment
or will you swell till you burst?

The victim has administered justice.

You move in accordance with my every change,
and you also are preserved; and while that ghastly light
still glows in you, you gather all our fragments.

(translated by Theo Hermans)

A TURKEY

Between the shrubs in the farmyard struts
the western domestic animal, digging in the clay
    for apple skins.

The dressed ape, the guard
    who tends himself in his fleshy husk,
    hatching an enormous egg all night long,
sees the turkey only as a feast for his saliva.

Yet no greedy hollowness puffed up this fowl,
the animal that speaks by day
    bred its fat.

Overfed by us
until the blood corals of its wattles
    swell with rage,
the turkey is as perfect an order
    as any one of Bach's 200 cantatas.

                    (translated by Theo Hermans)

A PIGEON

In the heraldry of moral rearmament
the dove figures as the bird of the soul
            seven spiritual gifts
            sacrifice of the poor.

    (The hen bird sits at night,
    the cock by day. Both
    have milk in their crops.)

Look at the white devil on the thawing ground,
nodding at the peat dust, his bed.

Listen how he coos, crueler than the kite and more in rut,
and you hear the wild ringdove in your wife's throat.

Monogamous?
Their guileless violence reduced
      to an emblem of duty,
their homely heat
      to a system for property.

(translated by Theo Hermans)

IN FLANDERS FIELDS

The soil here is superbly rich.
Even after all those years without manure
you could cultivate a dead man's leek here
to beat any market.

The shaky English veterans have dwindled.
Each year they point out to their dwindling friends:
Hill Sixty, Hill Sixty-One, Poelkapelle.

The combine harvesters in Flanders Fields describe
ever closer circles around the winding corridors
of hardened sandbags, the bowels of death.

The butter of this region
has a taste of poppies.

(translated by Theo Hermans)

The setting of this poem is the Belgian province of West Flanders, the site of pro-
longed and bitter trench fighting during World War I.—Editors' Note.

ISIS AND THE ANIMALS: 1

A rose clings to her skull
like a limpet, and her skull is

a cauliflower with feathers and skin
and illnesses and sorrow, and

in it there grows a golden pistil
which she loves to hold upright,

and like nightshade she goes,
with garlic in her hair,

towards the sound of gravel
where a child plays at knucklebones.

(translated by Theo Hermans)

AMBUSH

Crossing the plain, black with the ashes
of villages and woods
        (Their songs behind the hills:
        "We are the children of the wounded
        crocodile")
he walks, throbbing, throttled,
the weapon melting in his gloves.
        ("We are the children of the limping jackal")
He tries to march
towards his walkie-talkie,
        ("We are the children of the blind giraffe")
thinking: "I'm nothing but a conveyer of seed.
Nobody can laugh like me."

He has another three minutes to live.
Already above his helmet the deadly insect,
with rotor and sting, hangs in wait.
   ("We are the children of the wasp")

(translated by Theo Hermans)

Gust Gils
(1924–   )

HOW FINE N'EST-CE PAS

how fine n'est-ce pas the countryside on sunday
(morning beaming open promiseful
and later after noon all over the same
pairs in heat will go for a virtuous walk
their desire in need of lightning rods)

come do not fail to take an early trolley
you can kill yourself for free the woods are open
(gone the age of the gentleman's large estate)
no one to ask after you in a quiet nook
you will decay to utilitarian humus

and everything will go on happening
the man and his wife next door will celebrate
their porphyry wedding or something of the sort
there will be solar eclipses
and the saint in his sheet-iron single bed
will petrify in ice-cold visions

(translated by James S Holmes)

FAIRY TALE

the deer whose legs you try to hit
the nude girl with burning hair fleeing before you
at whom you shoot all your too-short arrows
and who will end up falling into your traps bleeding and
    panting

are more important to you no doubt
than the moving
but vague and far-off events
the queen who will quickly waste away and die
despite the precaution of a short nap
enjoyed beneath the immortality tree
from which she rose happy and hopeful,
dead queen who today is called eurythrocya
tomorrow pine-needle or something else
and whose death will always sadden
another king with a toothache
however quickly she is replaced.

but sometimes the deer inexplicably disappears
or it lures you into a lion's den
the virgin escapes in a wood full of thorns
or she lets her priceless once-in-a-lifetime membrane
be rent in the heat of another man's hayloft
then you remain behind purposeless and dejected,
a bottle without directions for use, a sandy plot
and you seek scant consolation at the dusty tomb
of the dead queen aldehyde
pine-branch or whatever she was called

(translated by Koos Schuur)

BALLAD OF A PERENNIALLY MISUNDERSTOOD MAN

when I, with the wind against me, happen to blow into a
    just-opened bottle of soda
or stumble up a perpendicular ladder carrying boots full of
    flour,
and my daughter laughs loudly and my father has plenty of
    good advice
left over,

when I work my tail off carrying baskets of peeled pears
up to the attic so they can dry,
or night after night help slovenly friends sort and order their
    masses of books
by subject,

whatever I do and however I do it—
always o for ten, so to speak,
which for that matter shows in the broad,

the well-paid, the dutiful smirk
of the City Control Officer: the man who always, every-
    where
manages to pass by at just the right moment.

                    (translated by Manfred Wolf)

TWO JAPANESE POEMS

I
the fujiyama
is quite a sight

but so am I
and twice to boot

said the girl
and she was right

2
the mayor of fukui
seems like a fervent zen buddhist to me
said I to the japanese guide
oh yes? said she
well anyway he kept talking
about the many zen buddhist shrines
in his city—are there? said I
oh yes said she
do we visit some of those? said I
oh no we won't have time for that
said she, are you interested in zen?
yes very said I
there are many zen buddhists
in japan said she
so I heard said I but I never got
to meet one in person
well neither did I said she

(written in English)

THE SWALLOWING OF THE EARTH

and everywhere great crowds
stood staring intently at the sky
at a gigantic cloud that looked
like a demon getting ready
to swallow the earth.

sporting shouts of approval resounded
when the monster
set its teeth in the planet.
but not for long, for what those watching saw
was nothing but the shadow

of what took place
in reality

(translated by James S Holmes)

THE FINE DIVINE MARQUIS

had the Marquis de Sade but been born
a couple of centuries later and so
still going strong, he'd have written
—for revenge no doubt, since even he
couldn't get rid of this riffraff
at his door—the lurid tale
I imagine of how one time
he invited one of those pairs
of female j.w.'s to come inside
and then, in the kind of debate
he was such a master at
prove to these frowsy creatures
the irrefutable grossness
of their Biblical errors.
after which, it hardly needs saying,
he'd proceed of course to seduce them
(with buggery first on the program)
and talk them into
trying out lesbian practices
not to mention the rest—
in brief, an orgy of inverted

proselytizing, after which the enlightened
pair, enthusiastic and nympho, would go
(witnessing in the name of De Sade)
from door to door, dispersing
the genuine doctrine of the divine Marquis
henceforward
in word and deed.

(translated by James S Holmes)

Hugues C. Pernath
(1931–1975)

SINCE DEW THE DAY

For my wife

The beginning explains since dew the day
My word that lives this narrow love,
I wrote the shame and deeply the hand
Her husky scream.
With five and holy older masters
The rubble violet, pure after that
Afternoon glory shall become her tongue.

The mintage in the edifice of the voice
After the refusal that stroking rules
Death, the birth of agony alone
No longer flows, signs hungrily
The wound of space. My brief name
This executioner's compassionate forehead
Bears her cross-breeding, the first original.

(translated by James S Holmes)

THE ANSWER IS

The answer is, grimly bearing of luxury
And night, the shell underground
Of hands excessive often. Spiteful mouth
Wisdom or shard, and shame the realm
This who is who engenders with alien youths.

Someone, as if I ever or ever
Would live outside my guilty climate, dying
In somber sovereign love, life after
And be Byan my son, of a father
Only the studded carat of midnight.

(translated by James S Holmes)

HE REPRESENTED A SKIN

He represented a skin, his enemy
The trapezium of winter, the account as if
The cry Remembrance served beloved the master
Closed safely round the sheath and sobbed
With the gibberish of scars
By the slow bedstead. In an extermination
Of error, finally drab resistance to the passion
For what was maimed, bore the right of beaks.

No knife no axe struck blossoms, the son
The stranger come with the riddle
Grandiose, in the thud of the horse's hooves
He reigned by the gates. Godliness broke a lover
Out of old age the heroes chiseled like mystery
And the water lay, time ringed in lies
Denial was and curse his fruitfulness.

(translated by James S Holmes)

From INDEX

31
This is a request, a realization.
This is the recognition of strangers and friends.
This is a differentiation.

To speak to someone after all.
After all to ask someone a question.

Yet, what should I ask?
What as a refugee?
What as a man?

I live, I look—
Or isn't this my world—
And underscore the sadness.
I listen and am condemned
To the lifelong notes of the Blue Blue Danube
Played:
As people were hanged
As people were gassed
As people were sterilized.
A night, of word and deed.
For the one who died at Dachau
Or laughs and lives, blindly free
At Petegem-on-the-Lys.

32
This is my world, the work of all.
Bravely we cling together, mobile and surprised.
And Flanders, my land, appoints itself plaintiff
And grimly apportions
Love and sorrow.

On a Friday the 16th of November 1860
Jan Coucke and Pieter Goethals
Were beheaded at Charleroi.
Possibly innocent.

Wasn't there one Fleming bilingual
Or capable of defending them?

Even a Pope speaks Dutch
When he's handed a Flemish bank check.

Like a swarm of flies on the blood sacrifice
We commit our annual, embittered desecration of graves.
And on the same plain of the Yser racism sprouts
From the fertile seed of a new pogrom.

The Flemish Authors' Guild
Holds its pilgrimage to Limburg
While a few miles further west
We shoot down our storks.

People like to watch the way things die.

33
We are prepared to forget our tradition.
We believe in little, for we know still less.
We own nothing,
But this is only a beginning.

A man among men,
We learned with words
What sin and murder were.
Since then so many voices have faltered,
The paltry disgrace has come, and all
That remains a shadow in the harmonious order
Of Treblinka, Hiroshima, Korea, Indonesia, or
Vietnam.

Man declares the death of man
And annihilates him in the name of memory.

In the name of the God who holds shares in
Standard Oil

Or is the crucified lover of one or another president.
And the foolish dove is still our only symbol.

34
Behold this life.
And in all honesty.
The seeing, the keeping silence.

For what is there still that could drive us mad?
What could tear out our eyes?

If I have no children
There are still the children of strangers
And of my friends.
For what we know of the bomb
Is hearsay merely.

O man, O friendly man
United by so many bonds
That prevent you
From living as you would.

After this no word has any importance.

(translated by James S Holmes)

Petegem-on-the-Lys is a village near the Flemish town of Deinze. It lies on the River
Leie, or Lys. The execution of Jan Coucke and Pieter Goethals became a *cause célèbre*
in nineteenth-century Belgium when it was learned that, while they as simple work-
ing-class Flemings could speak only their dialect of Dutch, their entire trial was pros-
ecuted by men (including even their defense counsel) who spoke only French. The
resultant furor in Flanders marked the beginning of the Flemish Movement against the
hegemony of French in Belgium. The annual desecration of graves and the sprouting
of racism on the Yser plain refer to an annual "pilgrimage" to the Yser area, the site
of some of World War I's most prolonged and bitter battles, by a large group of Flem-
ish militants, in which fascist and quasi-fascist elements play a not-unimportant part.
Limburg is a Dutch-speaking area in the east of Belgium (and the southeast of the
Netherlands).—Translator's Note.

UNCHASTITY

For Myra

Believe in me, for I believe in you
Refusing what was and knowing what held us back.
I shall rename you, bear you beyond this life
You, Only One, and shadow covering me.
Through you I have become, and with the scars
Upon your flesh, the sheen of you.

So our silences, so our speech.
Nothing was promised us, only the life
We chose can take us or abandon us,
No compassion, for nothing made us.

Because I saved my spittle for you, and now
After the Nacht und Nebel come alive again in your fears
And try to shield you against the horror.
No more complaint is needed, the pain has stilled
And settled. Only you and I germinate and flower
In the purifying mystery of tenderness.

Untoward lies our landscape, a tale of creation
In our seeking and our finding, the helpless, hopeless
Pursuit of the submission drawing out our bodies.
Purr. Purr and preserve me in your love.

So shall we be recorded, growing older than
The falcon that takes flight and traces wrinkles
Across the dry waste lands of previous and past.
No misunderstanding. Between you and me no survival
For this day meant for me the beginning of days.
You are my first day, I'm here, because I'm staying.

(translated by James S Holmes)

IN THE LOVELESS LANDSCAPE OF MY SOLITUDE

In the loveless landscape of my solitude
No soothing movement holds sway, no calm,
Comforting or finishing me off as a firstborn.
My haughty blood is translating the signs,
The flashes across the past's bitter pool,
Imbued with the qualities of one
Who eschews even the pains of November.
Wretched, denying flesh and dream, I retreat
Into my underworld of unbelief.

No limits, no beacons, no horizon.
Descending, like a one-track wanderer,
The falcon commences its fearsome flight.
And from the final remnants of my hope
Collecting the curious fragments of collapse,
Addicted and afterwards cured, I seek shelter
In the heinous havoc by which I'm consumed.

I shall do no damage, nor wreak destruction.
No sacred mountain is unknown to me,
I'll wish for a speedy recovery, peacefully
Trace the lifelines of remembrance back
To the scarcely smoldering ruins of my past,
And convulsed in my uprooted landscape
Will reach out for the shroud of deep sleep
Gently enough not to scratch open hate or pain
In her pregnantly lingering response of rejection.

(translated by Paul Vincent)

Paul Snoek
(1933–1981)

RUSTIC LANDSCAPE

The ducks are like our cousins:
they waggle and walk
and slavering at the mouth
In the mud grow old.

But all at once a terrific
bang almost breaks
their pleasant peasant membranes.

That was the farmer himself of course:
he's trying the shotgun out,
the lout. He cut an apple
In the snout and cried, stark red
with relief: "I'm dressing
yes, a golden pear."

And did those quacking cousins have a laugh.
(1) They prune their roses
with a crooked knife;
(2) How old are the ducks?

(translated by James S Holmes)

BALLAD OF A GENERAL

Red from glory and fat from defeats
washing himself with steaming water
the general stands in front of the window
of his only room.

The women of his career
cut at two sides,
for his stomach is hairy
with the kisses of swords.

Despondently, the general lets
his manly breasts, acquired
during a campaign in Europe,
hang resignedly.

Wet from water and red from Waterloo,
the general stands in front of
the only window of his room
drying himself with the tricolor.

(translated by John Stevens Wade)

The tricolor is in this case not the French flag (though there may be some Flemish
irony here) but the Belgian: red, yellow, and black.—Editors' Note.

SWEDISH ORGAN

A lot of girls lived in the castle
all year round
there were virgins living there too
but only in spring.

Though not at all dangerous at night
no one was allowed to go into the park.

Night was for burning the candles,
white with a smattering of red ones.

Then there was kissing and drinking.
They drank cool water at long tables.
And there was caressing music,
but it was cold and impressively strange.
It lacked the voice
of a man with a nightingale.

(translated by James S Holmes)

DUEL AMONG THE ROSES

We were agreed on the choice of weapons:
bursts of laughter.

We took our stance a foot apart
stripped to the waist despite the early hour
and in the presence of the doctor and the seconds
I burst into the first laugh.

But I soon had myself under control
and my opponent, a naval cadet,
bit right through his fine upper lip
so that his kiss on the mouth of the blonde
would never be the same again,
I was quite sure of that.
Oh, how that thought gave me courage.

And when a thick drop of blood trickled from his chin
and on the horizon appeared a coach
in which without doubt only in black silk
and fine underclothes sat the blonde,
his final hour had struck.

I let out an infectious chuckle
which toppled him groaning into the roses,
hardy yellow dwarf roses actually,
in an uncontrollable fit of laughter.

Even when the doctor was doing his examination
he lay there squirming indescribably.

The seconds led him cautiously away.

The fine blonde sat sobbing deliciously
and on a patch of lawn, fresh and dewy,
not far from the trampled roses,
I soon made her mine.
Oh boy.

(translated by Alasdair MacKinnon)

END OF THE ICE AGE

On an ascent of Annapurna
a British expedition discovered,
12,000 feet up in an ice cave,
the frozen-in body
of an abominable snowman.

They sawed a block of the ice out
and flew the body in a deep-freeze to London,
where today it is being unfrozen
and examined in the presence of several professors.

The BBC is transmitting the event in color
and in the heat of the TV spots
the ice starts melting quickly.
Most of the professors are wearing rubber boots
as they are almost ankle deep in water.

The body is now gradually appearing.
The skin is yellow and wrinkled
and sticky as a newborn baby.
You can sniff the sweet smell of a placenta.

Two professors first measure the skull circumference
and take samples of all fluids.
They are delighted to establish
that the heart, after a seven-hundred-year standstill
is once more beginning to beat
and that the snowman, although with difficulty, is breathing
and his thawed lungs have thus made contact with the air.

Then his lips begin to quiver,
he opens his mouth convulsively,
two professors do a quick tooth count
and into a microphone, held up by an interviewer
on its chrome-plated support,

the snowman clears his throat
and stammers out before millions of viewers:
Sumer is icumen in
Lhude sing cuccu!

(translated by Alasdair MacKinnon)

In the original the thawed snowman speaks the lines "Hebban olla vogala nestas ha-gunnan, / Hinase ic anda thu" (All the birds have begun their nests, / Except for me and you), usually considered the oldest text in Dutch.—Editors' Note.

PANIC ON THE OIL RIG

They have stopped drilling since yesterday.
In the particular circumstances it is better
to let the pipes and the drill rust
as the whole team are going around drunk

in dirty yellow jerkins
among a hundred or more journalists.

A Navy helicopter
has just let down a zoologist and a reporter
in the murky brown water of the North Sea
on the spot where seven frogmen, dropped last night,
come up for air
to their inflatable orange dinghy.

Nothing has been traced yet, though one young bloke,
who twenty-four hours ago
was still welding pipes together, swore by God,
that he saw two of them swimming around.

Science is baffled
since it has proved
that all life in the North Sea has died out.
Even the codfish.

(translated by Alasdair MacKinnon)

SAY IT WITH VEGETABLES

It is time to put a stop once for all
to this frivolous sentimental flower cult.
Too many plants are neglected
not to say rooted out
and damn it there are other things growing on this earth
besides tulips, roses, and daisies.

For example take the ridiculous custom
of forcing an expensive bouquet into the hands of the bride
who's no virgin now anyway
and sticking posies all over the reception table.

From now on let the bride carry a hard asparagus stem
and on the table put a bit of spinach as well
and give the gentlemen at most a shallot in their buttonholes.

Don't you think it's pathetic too
to see the world champion on his podium
after the playing of his national anthem
waving some deadly dangerous bunch of flowers?
If people would only pay tribute to these chaps
with a good bunch of leeks or celery.
Vegetable soup contains more vitamins than you think.
Or is it that for all their doping
they still don't look pale enough, maybe?

Florists ought to be closed down too
and all varieties of roses destroyed.
In their gardens people should grow nothing
but proper stinging nettles and wild grass.
In particular the cultivation of the blue thistle
should be encouraged by state subsidy
among all sections of the population.

And if here or there in some village
there's still some poetic type going around
for whom spring just isn't spring without sowing
he can always apply to the authorities.

They will smile and provide him with the necessary:
a plastic packet full of plastic seeds.

(translated by Alasdair MacKinnon)

OXYGEN FOR A CASTLE IN THE AIR

Women should be beautiful and fly a lot.
Move with unfolded, unspeaking wings
when I sleep in the moon's cradle
or stay among vivid sails
on one of this earth's seven seas.

High above the towers of my dreams
they should float with elegance
and turned-off engines,
when I inhabit my castle
and work at the secrets of distance.

Because no one will ever control
the flywheel's fancy the way I do.
Because there is silence in the air
I'm in a position to write: Lindbergh
has found the black box of Icarus.
Dear audience, I promise you solemnly
long-lasting fireworks
one hour before and one hour after my death.

(translated by Peter Nijmeijer)

TO STAY ALIVE

Why am I tired of this life?
In the morning a panting storm
hangs in the lungs of the weather.
In the afternoon I must kill flies
and in the evening chase away mosquitoes.

What do I hear in my dreams when I sleep?
A rustling among the tiles.
There's a rat in my roof again,
a sleek otter which in my attic
is gnawing away at the beams.

This misery lasts a whole day.
A white swallow flies off like ink,
the spider sits cursing in her trembling web
and the sun will no longer go down.
But I'm ready for anything.

(translated by Claire Nicolas White)

THE SIXTIES: GROUNDING REALITY

. . . the best
poems get written while peeling potatoes
   —CEES BUDDINGH', "Ars Poetica"

what lithely springs in the corner
of an eye
in one ear out the other
is not
the background music of frogs
but the poem itself . . .
   —J. BERNLEF, "The Sound of Matter"

. . . no metaphors
but material I rummage in
  losing a blinder here
  an association there
till what surrounds and pervades me
makes speechless . . .
   —J. BERNLEF, "The Sound of Matter"

the size of a child's shoe is a poem . . .
   —K. SCHIPPERS, "Bianca's First Steps in the Arts"

Cees Buddingh'
(1918–   )

PHYSICS

"o, is that what they think!"
said the boy
reading newton's law

and he soared like a lark
in the damp fall sky
and no mortal on earth
ever saw him again

(translated by James S Holmes)

ARS POETICA

I can remember it as if it were only yesterday:
I was perhaps 22: I sat
brooding over a poem, while my mother
sat at the window peeling potatoes.

the poem wouldn't work out: the sweat
was running down my back and, annoyed, I thought:
how in the name of god the father can a man write

poems in a room where someone
is sitting peeling potatoes?

that evening, when everyone was asleep, I finished
my poem. It was an exceedingly bad one
and only much later I realized: the best
poems get written while peeling potatoes

(translated by James Brockway)

STEP BY STEP

much remains hidden, but much much
is revealed to us:

the structure of the atom
the rules for volleyball
sophia loren's breasts
the death of bird the birth of trane
the latest fashion in spacesuits
the simple use of the crumb brush

with briefcases full of darkness
we walk in a knifesharp light

(translated by James S Holmes)

HISTORICAL MATERIALISM

tonight, on the balcony
while I was shaking out the tablecloth
two backyards further on I suddenly

saw in the three-quarters darkness
six white shirts
neatly pinned to the clothesline

it gave me the same kind of shock
as the six manifestations
of lenin atop a piano
in the well-known painting
by salvador dali

(translated by James S Holmes)

PETIT SALON DES INDÉPENDANTS

I'm willing to go along quite a way
with him and him, and also
with this one, that one, and the other:
but always reserving the right
e.g., when everyone's raving
about sexus, plexus, and nexus, to say
give me horatio alger,
or when free verse is all the rage,
to publish a sonnet

(and vice versa)

(translated by James S Holmes)

THE MUSIC MAKERS

true, nature is wonderful,
with its lovely green trees, its lovely colored flowers,
and its many, many birds with their gems of song—

yet:
give me man,
the only animal in creation
that devours its own kind
and in between meals
puts on a record by joseph haydn

(translated by James S Holmes)

SUFFICIENT UNTO THE DAY

This morning after breakfast
I discovered in my groping way
that the lid of the marmite pot
(4 oz. net, medium size)
exactly fit the small bottle of heinz sandwich spread

of course I tried at once
to fit the lid of the sandwich spread
on the marmite pot

and it fit yes it did

(translated by Elizabeth Willems-Treeman)

SHOPPING

last week I stopped by the grocer's
because wiebe had phoned and asked me
to buy a pot of jam: cherry
(but that was sold out: there *was* strawberry)

while I was paying the grocer said:
"by the way, that lid doesn't fit
on a bottle of sandwich spread"

so you see: slowly but surely poetry
is reaching the right people after all

(translated by James S Holmes)

THE MONKEY

Our closest relative, but how far we have
    outgrown him! When we really want a good laugh
we cluster round his cage: watch him tumble and squirm,
tease his brothers and sisters, scoot away, settle down to
    finely flea himself and oh, the grubby comic,
gobbling down the fleas like extremely dainty hors d'oeuvres!

The very idea! How quaint! Yes, if only
    man is sure enough that he is superior
he's willing to be sentimental: in this case even the dullest
dolt can nurture the illusion of his supremacy:
    even if he had to repeat every grade,
he's still a creature—thank you—of a much higher order.

And it's true: you can't teach a monkey much: stacking
    boxes, selecting
    from circles and triangles, black, white, or brown,
pulling a pointer out into a longer one—that's about it:
he has no vocal center and besides his frontal brain
    is somewhat underdeveloped—and hence
unlike us he knows nothing of morals or ethics.

He's simply a sitter, a hanger, an eater,
    which we're glad to accept of any other animal;

but in his case, with whom we share a common forefather
    . . .?
Is there still the same possibility in us? Is Secretary (no
    names, please) who not long ago spoke so movingly
of duty and sacred calling, perhaps still one-sixteenth mon-
    key?

So he keeps on posing us problems, the ugly primate!
    while he himself goes on frolicking through the jungle;
well, frolicking: he's got troubles of his own; who knows,
maybe there's a leopard on the lookout for him in the tree
    over there, children too can be a bother sometimes, and
    that fat
rival is always hovering just a little too close round his ha-
    rem.

In front of his cage again. "Liz, 'd you see the monkeys eat
    their dinner?"
"What? with a knife?"—Glass quivers, branches crack.
At Cape Kennedy they fasten the helmet of his spacesuit.
I stare into two black, bottomless pools.
    A child's voice cuts the air. If there were no monkeys
I'd be more satisfied with creation.

(translated by James S Holmes)

ODE TO THE YORKSHIRE DALES

Every man, even the most doubting Thomas,
still retains some kind of vision of paradise:
for me that is the part of England between
Ingleton and Leyburn, Grassington and Hawes:
when I'm there I'm inclined to think: yes, the world
    must have a divine origin.

Which is nonsense, of course: millions of folk
would say: What? all those hills, those barren moors?
not a luscious chick in sight, just dumb sheep,
what a musty, deadly, grayish solitude.
I'd utterly pine away here with a week—and
     you call this a garden of Eden?

But with paradises it's just about the same
as with love: the one blows his brains out
for a creature whom another would rather
see dead in a ditch: when I think
of the myriad hordes on the Costa del Sol, then
     it makes *my* hair stand on end.

This, of course, remains a matter of infantile
desires, fears, illusions: our first three years
have a lot on their conscience in this matter too—
when you adore both space and intimacy,
experiencing emptiness as splendor and bustle as emptiness,
     you're ripe for the Yorkshire Dales.

Everything is slightly grayish, dusty, veined
with browns and hazy blues, even spring looks
like autumn there—a frightfully beautiful landscape,
though not friendly, rather surly, self-contained,
a landscape like a man who never pats you on the shoulder
     but on whom you can always depend.

Thus it shows that even in your own little paradise
you end up looking for yourself: the image of an ideal
superego, dear and obliging to your id, a kind
of father and mother in one, who'll never desert you—
O donkeys of Arncliffe, when again shall I see you
     grazing upon your *green?*

          (translated by Peter Nijmeijer)

SOMETIMES, IN THE EVENING

Sometimes, in the evening, my father appears in the room.
Become strangely old, almost skin and bone.
"They sleeping, Stientje and the boys?" "O yes."
(They mustn't see him.) He sighs contentedly.

"They doing all right? No sicknesses?" "No, no sicknesses
fortunately. Everything's okay." He smiles,
small on the edge of the seat, his legs
even shorter than when he was a boy.

We don't speak, but nod "chin up"
as before. "I'd better be going. Aye lad." He stands
briefly before an early photo of my mother.

The garden gate squeaks. I listen to his steps,
those featherlight, booming steps
of someone who must return to the dead.

(translated by Anthony Akerman)

J. Bernlef
(1937–   )

THE SOUND OF MATTER

what lithely springs in the corner
of an eye
in one ear out the other
is not
the background music of frogs
but the poem itself
product of my imagination
just as my shoes
are a product of Bata

"Imaginary gardens
with real toads in them"
to wit, no metaphors
but material I rummage in
    losing a blinder here
    an association there
till what surrounds and pervades me
makes speechless

I gauge my blindness
    with my eyes
my deafness
    with my ears:

the sound of matter
falling
on the retina

(translated by James S Holmes)

ERIK SATIE

Like a sledge through snow
like a wiggling little finger
like a storm in a forgotten red-label
teacup
3 x "like" and still haven't said
who Satie is
who was too young
for this world of old hat.

I put on his *Sports et Divertissements*
20 demonstrations of daintiness
and write
like an elderly lady in a playground
like birds' toes in fresh earth
like dooh like dah
my daughter screams
and yah
c'est çah
c'est Satie.

(translated by Theo Hermans)

UNCLE CARL: A HOME MOVIE

Saw a home movie today. Uncle Carl
caught unawares in a small boat near the lakes.
Three weeks later he was dead, no longer susceptible to
celluloid.

How good it would be to have a movie of his dying
the projectionist, reeling off his last breath
in slow motion the fogging of his eyes the falling of that
hand along the iron bedstead, showing it again and again.

Or at top speed, so that Uncle Carl's dying
would take on something merry, a rollicking dance on a
creaking bed
the embrace of an invisible woman

who kisses him awake on the rewind; the eyes
again turn their gaze, looking into the lens, the hand point-
ing.
Uncle Carl is alive, Uncle Carl is dead.

(translated by Scott Rollins)

THE ART OF BEING SECOND

Right behind the leader slipped into the byway
(which he had overlooked)
and so came upon the currant bush.

All right, they taste bitter but
in the long run you get used to everything.

Small, hard berries, sour
but tasting sweet next to the
leader's already half-decayed body.

(translated by Peter Nijmeijer)

DELIGHT

The horse almost in the room
its whinny like a wild
singing for quiet things
at the open window

The round coffeecups stand empty
the saucers gleaming in morning light
tremors pass through the glasses
in knives sharp and pointed right

At first sight order seems
to rule, regularity, till
it's standing there, as I said almost
in the room its white breath snorts

It grazes beside our breakfast
quick, with fierce tugs tufts of grass
it has no reproach for us but that delight
is not so fragrant and green as it once was.

(translated by James S Holmes)

K. Schippers
(1936–   )

BIANCA'S FIRST STEPS IN THE ARTS

The boundaries of the plastic arts
have been extended (Duchamp):
a shoe is an art object

The boundaries of music
have been extended (Cage):
creaking of shoes is music

The boundaries of ballet
have been extended (Cunningham):
walking is dance

The boundaries of poetry
have been extended (Buddingh'):
the size of a child's shoe is a poem

Bianca—age 1½
walks through the room
in her first pair of shoes

(translated by Peter Nijmeijer)

JIGSAW PUZZLES

Make a jigsaw puzzle from an amateur photo:
a large one or a small one

Make a very difficult jigsaw puzzle
from a simple text—
carefully sawing the pieces,
first pasting the paper on plywood

Jigsaw puzzles of famous paintings
completed or not, in a museum or in a closet

Photos of what?:
small and large sizes

Make jigsaw puzzles from jigsaw puzzles
(large and small)

Photograph a completed jigsaw puzzle
and make a jigsaw puzzle from that

Or photograph thousands of jigsaw pieces
—scattered—and make a jigsaw puzzle from that

Also simple jigsaw puzzles—two pieces

A large jigsaw puzzle with just a few pieces

Very small ones in a lot
Very small ones in a few

Surprise someone on his birthday
with a plain box containing
his portrait sawed into jigsaw pieces

Transform the white museum walls
into a white, completed jigsaw puzzle
which encloses the other jigsaw puzzles
—the paintings, etc.—

So, in fact, making a problem
out of everything

Jigsaw puzzles in one piece:
a whole without pieces

Exhibit all these jigsaw puzzles in a museum
or keep them in a closet

(translated by Peter Nijmeijer)

A BRICKBAT FOR KRAZY KAT

Someone doesn't like rubber bands.
He sees a beautiful box.
Would his evaluation of that box change
if he knew it contained rubber bands?

Someone doesn't like yellow.
But he does like green.
Green is partly yellow.
Does he like yellow after all?

(translated by Peter Nijmeijer)

GRAINS OF SAND ON A RADIO

A collection of umbrellas:
that's something.

A collection of cups
on a table in a lobby:
that's something less.

A collection of houses, hair, grains of sand,
leaves, drops of water:
that's nothing.

But think of the décor.

When you spot a collection of umbrellas
in an umbrella shop, you don't
think: "Look at that."

And grains of sand and leaves
become something again
on a polished floor
or—especially—on a radio.

A cup standing by itself
in a bookcase or
on the edge of a small table
is more quickly noticed than
a lot of cups together.

We don't usually tolerate
such isolation for long:
it is put with the others.

But collections
do not rule us.

We can generally
make do with a series
of a single sample.

(translated by Peter Nijmeijer)

HOW A GUITAR CAN LIE ON A CHAIR

There it is on a kitchen chair,
not even particularly askew,
ready for chording or casing
or to be recognized.

Notice with how little
an observer can make do:
some length of its strings,
bit of curve of its body,
angle of the bridge, two, three pegs,
four letters of its maker's name.

I must have seen it
from a different angle too:
quietly by itself in a shopwindow or
on a stage with someone next to it,
hence I can fill out
enough of its shape
in the kitchen—ample fragments
for the whole of the guitar.

Looking is adding up in good faith:
this is the front of the spoon,
so there should be a back also.
under the tabletop
there are legs,

a door and not even the thought
that someone in the hall
might open it.

(translated by Peter Nijmeijer)

Armando

(1929–   )

TRIP WITH KNIVES

a man travels (eyes head and face of the servingmen
who it is true pay no gold, so
I have to pull apart)
like a wonder.
thus you agree, now hear, to this land:
a nation with consciences and knives.
uncertain and helpful,
he feels humiliated.

he quickly sails with crew across Blade.
one pull: the 5 fingers are loose now, have their own lives.
are you asleep? are you singing?
there's no problem now with the wounds,
the 5 fingers are loose now!
life begins now, another life: i am a ruler.

(translated by James S Holmes)

THE SHIP! THE WHITE SHIP!

the ship! the white ship! sails through the houses,
sails against my world, against the animals,
water over the world.

they walk, they run, they have the largest hands.
glass anchor, yelling anchor.
"ruler no longer, ruler no more!"

the ship! the fast ship!
water in the animals, in the earth.
is no servingman is no master, is no ruler.
ships approach. dead ships?
ships with teeth? ships with nails?
"rule no longer, rule no more."

(translated by James S Holmes)

BOXERS

for Hans Sleutelaar

does nelis have a glass chin?
●

get 'im right in the gullet
dammit-to-hell no breath left

●

, a feint a couple of teasers
me from the left him from the right
i get inside i catch 'im
he's flat on his ass for 3 red ones,

●

say: loosen my gloves. water.
says: show self-control.
say: loosen my gloves. water.
says: show self-control.
say: fuck off with your self-control. water.

(translated by James S Holmes)

Hans Sleutelaar was, with Armando, in the forefront of the New Style movement of
the early sixties.—Translator's Note.

Judith Herzberg
(1934–   )

KITTEN

How did it know where I was standing?

Bleeding from its cut ears
the animal dragged itself blind
zigzag over gravel
to where I
wildly hoping against reason
stood.

In any event, they considered
the tail had to be cut.
So I gave her up for that.

She was strange, stuffed with death—
I eased her into the earth

my shiny childcat
shortlived relative
versatile butterflycat.

And avoided the barn
after finding the tail there
a week later.

(translated by the author)

There was a superstitious belief in the north of Holland (where I was in hiding as a
child during the war) that a particular cats' disease could be cured by bleeding the cat,
as described in this poem.—Author's Note.

MAGIC

Before the war all that was different—
boxes full of pointed Caran d'Ache
in all the colors of the rainbow
but if you slid them open
everything changed because
before the war there was a war at hand.

Look how sweet children
look how sweet we were
we locked our mother into the cellar
we blew up frogs with a straw.

And when we slid those boxes open
fireworks jumped out on parachutes
that were shot down at once
and, falling, striped the sky.

So it was all
our own fault
as she often used to say.

(translated by the author)

AFTER A PHOTO

*From a photograph of a fifteen-year-old actress, taken after a
first night*

She hears, head empty,
what he knows about life.
She keeps his story whole
by not sorting it out.

She lets his words come in
calmly. She comes from the calm
from the calm childhood
her understanding is taking in.

With the seriousness too of a child
that allows everything: ill luck, pain
just because it is there
and she begins at the beginning
no final point in mind.

She keeps his story in one piece
by not wishing to match it with another
comparing it to something that resembles
and yet doesn't quite resemble.

Actually more serious than he
with his scornful jokes
about what he hardly dares call sadness
or injury
she allows him to laugh
and waits till he has finished laughing.
Head empty, tired, affectionate.

                              (translated by the author)

BURYING

Would he understand that I wasn't at his grave
because I had a cold, if I had a cold?
And would he recognize this as a pretext
nod at me a yes naturally, and that it
wasn't necessary at all? That it was no use to hear
this rain on his coffin, that he himself

wouldn't be here if he didn't happen—
He with his little table lamp foldable scissors thermostat.
Who kept doors closed against the draft, his eyes open
especially for the unfolding of young leaves
his ears just for the brightening twitter
of birds in the aviary—Would he
understand, if he still understood at all,
what brought me here, under these improperly hurried
clouds, while he was unable to attend?

(translated by the author)

VOCATION

And when they asked her what she wanted to be
she said "Invalid" and saw herself,
legs motionless in brownish plaids,
pushed by devoted husband and pale sons;
not even a stamp to paste herself,
not a letter to write, no trip to take.
Then she would be really free at last,
look as sad as she pleased, take her
turn before others in stores, be up
in front at parades, no pretty clothes,
and every night sobbing softly
she would say, "Not on account of myself
but all that trouble for you."
And both boys would always
stay with her, devote
their lives to her, and nothing
would ever happen to her,
never, never would she wear out.

(translated by Manfred Wolf)

YIDDISH

My father sang the songs
(which his mother used to sing)
for me, who half understood them.

I sing the same words again;
nostalgia flaps in my throat,
nostalgia for what I have.

Sing for my children
what I don't understand myself,
so that they later . . . Later?

Before the roses are faded
we drink the flowers' water.

Sad, intimate language,
I'm sorry that you withered
in this head.
It no longer needs you
but it does miss you.

(translated by Manfred Wolf)

A CHILD'S MIRROR

"When I grow old I will have blond curls.
I won't have thick blue veins, no double chin,
and when I get wrinkles because I am fifty
they'll be cheerful ones, not deep lines at my mouth
just a few crow's-feet around my eyes.

"I'm never going to lie or cheat, why should I
and no one is ever going to lie to me.
I'm not going to have those greasy

gray strands of hair and I am certainly not going
to smell dreadfully from my mouth.

"I'll have a dog three cats and a goat
who is allowed indoors, I think that's cozy,
and never mind the droppings.
The cats may sleep with me in bed
the dog sleeps on the rug.

"I'll have beautiful plants full of flowers
none of those dull stalks and certainly no insects.
I'll have a very loving husband who is quite famous
the whole day and also the whole night
we will stay together all the time just the two of us."

(translated by the author)

BEAR IN BED

PRAGUE (A.F.P.)—A farmer living by himself in the Tatra
Mountains on the Polish-Czechoslovak border has harbored a
bear for several months. One day he found the animal in his
bed. All efforts to dislodge it failed. The next morning the bear
left, well-rested, to forage, only to return at night and stretch
out again on the farmer's bed. It kept this up for several months,
but now the bear has disappeared. The mountain dweller fears
it has been shot by a poacher. *(Het Parool,* February 12, 1962)

Ah yes, I had a bear,
a bear had me, and for the first
time in my house someone
was having his way. In the dark
I came home from chopping wood,
pulled off my boots in the corner
where I sleep, but it stank
strange, of animal.

It was a fat, wet fur
but no, it grumbled.
There was no budging it.
An uncomfortable night.

In the morning
on his way out
he drank my week's supply
of sour milk,
licked the bottom clean
upsetting the bucket,
and then stepping carefully over it.

It was roomy when he had gone.

In the evening he came back,
shook himself dry
the drops hissed in the fire.

Good evening, I said.
He stepped lightly again,
only the rap rap
of his nails on clay.

Tell me what you did
today, have you eaten
did you hunt?

For the first time someone
in that house had his way:
lay down, fell asleep.

I was up already
sitting on the doorstep
when he came outside
with his small discontented eyes.

The sun shone
and the bear disappeared
in the direction of Zilina.

At night he came home,
I gave him new milk
I'd fetched in the valley
and asked: What did you do?
Meet a she-bear?

He moved into my life
staying on and on,
and I'll never find out
what else he did.

I was sharpening my axe
in the yard to store
wood for the winter when a hawk
circled over our heads.

Traitor, ally, spy?

The bear got a message
without looking up.
He waited awhile,
then spinning around

loosely on his easy legs
he lumbered into the wood
and disappeared.

How could he leave,
not wanting to stay
after coming to sleep every day?

I searched in the woods,
but all God's dumb bucks

all dried-up brooks
blown-off branches
cloud stripes and rock cracks
pointed the wrong way.

Then the first snow came
and I gave up,
stumbled back in the cold
hoping without hope
I'd find him at home.

Where did he come from?
Is that where he'd gone?
How can I save him
from traps or whatever
if he's not where I've searched
two nights and two days?

Shot, dragged half dead
through the snow,
maybe bought and already
sold.

(translated by Shirley Kaufman)

SNEAKERS

Just got used to
the tearing down of houses
the stooping over of uncles
yet more stooped in the coming years
putting away twelve-year-old
airedales, used to, I mean

not so much the senseless wearing out
as: "it's had its day."
Not so much one's own death then,
in disguise of someone else's,
as the end of certain mainstays
which last shorter than we do, or started
earlier. No one is attached to a strawberry.
But this is shaky ground
because if you really start thinking about a strawberry
really, in the way you can also begin to
think about a spider after he's fallen three times
in the same pail and you've rescued him three times
(the first time because you didn't want a dead
spider in the water, the second time
because you did it the first time and the third
because you know him)
well, just got used to the wilting I was going to say
when suddenly I got a pair of sneakers
exactly like the ones I had ten years ago. The same
faces, color, design, laces—
So absolutely the same that a second life
didn't seem ruled out. Astonished, I see them walk
but with my legs, my ankles, my feet.

(translated by Scott Rollins)

TREE SURGEON

Tree surgeon he called himself, and with his power saw
he was sitting high up in my tree when you put your bike
against the fence. Always and by nature
against pruning you just said: "So . . ." and I saw
that something was the matter with you.

"I think something is growing inside me that does not be-
      long there."
That same moment a branch fell so that the roof
of the shed broke. I ran away
and didn't know until that night what it was like for you—
worries broke out in me, not to be stopped,
about if we ever lost each other
and how, before it gets that far, we'll
plod stupidly ahead, and only when the creaking
becomes really frightful will we trot helpfully
in the wrong direction.

                    (translated by Ria Leigh-Loohuizen)

THE DISHWASHER

to my cutlery

Farewell knives and forks, I'll never wash you again.
This is the end of our affair. No more fond chitchat
between soft linen. I'll bundle you into a crèche like
troublesome children. I'm glad to have had you, couldn't
bear to part with you, but your familiar features
won't pass through my hands again.
My little charges; as of now you're just dirty dishes.
Listen, let's be reasonable. They just won't do,
these conversations after breakfast: was the porridge
all right, did the egg leave stains, did they bite too
hard on you and was the rhubarb refreshing?

And my rickety-rackety lopsided baby, my
sweet tiny spoon, must you be rinsed with the rest?

Ah, noble soup ladle, will your offspring henceforth
be rudely drenched without regard to rank?

Let's not kid ourselves. Of course you understand
the age of putting things to soak is past.
Our days are filled with weightier affairs.
Personalities in need of development, like mine,
just don't have time to wash by hand.

(translated by John Rudge)

Rutger Kopland
(1934–   )

JOHNSON BROTHERS LTD.

Back then, my father still big,
dangerous tools bulging his pockets,
a strong smell of tow and lead in his suits,
behind his eyes the incomprehensible
world of a man, a first-class pipefitter
said mother. How different I must have felt
back then when he closed the doors
on her and on me.

Now he is dead, and I suddenly as old
as he, amazed that into him, too, decay
could have been built. Among his notes I find
appointments with strangers, on his wall
calendars with a maze of beautiful gaspipes,
on the mantelpiece the portrait of a woman
in Paris, his wife, the incomprehensible
world of a man.

Looking in the little porcelain sink
from the Thirties with the two clumsy lions
holding up their shield: Johnson Brothers Ltd.,
high up in the stone-still house mother's sad shuffle
Jesus Christ, father, tears

for now and for then, flowing
together in the lead gooseneck
becoming one with the drops
from the little brass tap marked COLD.

(translated by Ria Leigh-Loohuizen)

OLD COUNTRY HOUSE

It used to be so beautiful.

But Her Ladyship with the lovely ass
has disappeared into the meadows
with the gardener, in search of the secrets
of the birds and the bees, she said.

The gamekeeper has shot the last
nightingales for the mantelpiece. All they do is
keep you awake, he said.

Nests hang, naked and open
in the trees. For everybody to see.

And in the night a cow stumbles
like an old poet out of the canal
lit by her mate the moon
and deposits on the steps her plopping
message of freedom.

(translated by Ria Leigh-Loohuizen)

YOUNG LETTUCE

I can take it all,
the withering of beans,
flowers dying, with dry
eyes I can see the potatoes being
dug up, when it comes
to those, I'm really tough.

But young lettuce in September,
just planted, still limp,
in little moist beds, no.

(translated by Ria Leigh-Loohuizen)

AMONG THE FLOWERS

She let him see it. Still completely bare
and bald and not yet actually
mysterious. She giggled.

Diana caught by Pluto in the
flower patch, first from the side, and after
from behind. He thrust and jerked

convulsively. As big as a finger,
among the matches, pennies, cigarette stubs
it began to come alive. All at once

he was hanging there on her backside like
a child, and wanted to run, run.

(translated by James S Holmes)

BLACKBIRD

The way you start to sing when you get
slowly horny. So sweet and so gentle
it would always

with your breasts against my chest
and between us nothing more nothing
else but that

would it always have been a kiss on stone,
a cold breeze, against it a blackbird

gentle sweet friend of mine. The way
I can smell your breath this is
what cunt meant

it wouldn't be lost but
just never have been. Listen

blackbird, are you there, between
my legs, take these broken
hands and learn

to write how your hair falls down and
your head rocks and I feel you
moan and sing

high above my skylight, blackbird
against the cold air, against the sun,
against me.

(translated by Ria Leigh–Loohuizen)

NO GENERATION

Everyone everywhere always
we too arrived at that point
where we didn't belong to any generation,
we were in it alone

by the fire, the air above
green from the leaves
raining little gray flakes
into the gin, and the half-dead butterflies
still struggling, everything came
together, and then drinking, drinking

so there was a younger and an older
generation, and a no-generation:
we, who couldn't see anything else

but us, not free, not bound, just . . .
what? That feeling. It was up to us
and we weren't up to it.

Of course we were without
the excuses that bring all differences back
to other differences

and we thought of each other the way you
can think at night together, of never
nowhere nobody.

(translated by Ria Leigh-Loohuizen)

TARZAN ONCE MORE

He had to be brown and in heat, soft men
dreamed him up; their fantasy
nourished by apes with bananas, yes he

still remembers the script, Help me
she said, the moist young woman, while
he looked over her shoulder, far away, and protective

and saw again the Big Mission, the Sacrifice, the sense
of his existence. And so, each night
he was raped by the women.

Lonely, but happy with him, and only with him,
all of them; real men were rare then,
life was still hard and without poetry.

Oh, if only he could say goodbye to her once more,
she would cry: Stay, stay! and he could fumble
with his knife, and go away, away into the jungle.

                    (translated by Ria Leigh-Loohuizen)

G

G, I wrote a poem about your face,
that it was so absent, I compared it
to water that I can see the face of
a horse in, and when I looked up

the opposite bank was empty. I compared
it to wind that I can hear the breath in
of a dead dog, and when I listened
it was so goddamned still in the house.

I compared it, G, to much
more, more than I remember, but
I can't find the poem again.

It wasn't just water, wind, you see
me even when I don't look, you breathe when
I don't listen, read what I don't write.

                              (translated by James S Holmes)

CONVERSATION

I
The sounds of freight trains, the old
stories of the night, that they're coming
to get you, that they will take you with them,
but what remains is no more than
the rustling that's always there,

or the gray of a windstill sea in
the evening, maybe underneath there is
still a very slow breathing, but
you can't see it, a sleep
so deep, so for good, as long

as you live, something like that, she says. And I who
never wanted these conversations, who never have
had an answer, because I, too,
don't know a name for what I don't
hear and don't see, but am lying

now against her body, I think of her
as if she were a child that isn't a child
any more, of the sounds of

the night, the color of the old
summers by the sea.

II
Or she says nothing, is only silent.
It is true, farther and farther away
the soft freight trains disappear into the night,
they came to get me, but I didn't go, I stay
and listen until I hear nothing any more.

Or she is dead still, it is as if she's asleep.
I see her lying, and indeed in her
body lives the secret of the swaying
in a windstill sea. I keep on
looking until I see nothing any more.

There is, I say, and I think, it isn't there.
The words I use to say: there has been a time
and it has gone now, there is
a place and this, too, is deserted,
they are consolation, but for what.

Not for what has been, but for later:
I hear, but the silence after,
I see, but what is no more,
I think, but about what.

(translated by Ria Leigh-Loohuizen)

DEAD BIRDS

I
Why have these dead birds,
why particularly now
they are dead,

those pheasants and partridges,
why have they been put there on damask,
against velvet curtains, among chestnuts, grapes,
goblets of wine?

You think you know, you see.

Around those small eyelids, still
that fear of being visible, still
that hope of disappearing
in the heather, the edge of the forest.

II
And why all that sand, that sky,
that sea, that gray
end of the world?

If that seagull wasn't living there,
in the corner of the photograph,
with spread wings on the beach, still
that attempt to fly away, still
that hope of disappearing
in all that gray.

III
Why then. Although you know,
you forget

—this painting, this photograph,
this rich table, this empty beach—

that they only are what you see.

After the fear of being seen,
the hope of disappearing,
after those are gone,

they are lying there, things now
among the things.

(translated by Ria Leigh-Loohuizen)

H. C. ten Berge
(1938–   )

SONG ENCOUNTERED IN THE LANDSCAPE

Niko pirosmanashvili is my name
and they pestered me to death
for too long now I've been watching a man in the snow
an exquisite harmonica player who dances
as he plays

snow that shines a white-
hot image
in my eyes
now that father sun recovers from his seven matings
I mean

that dazzled me blind
and haughtily withdraws into the wind

they think I'm insane
for the children can be heard from way off
as they come seizing apples
for the winter there are apples on my tree
any fruit can readily be captured here

therefore I watch a man in the snow
who carries music and colors

his sound with soft brushes
niko pirosmani is my name
and they pestered me to death

bear that well in mind.

(translated by Theo Hermans)

GREENLAND FOSSIL / AN ICY POET

Sun fine old fellow
chasing females on other planets

the cold rides his body
like hoary crossbeams,
the needles pierce
the petrified backside of language

foundations of poetry
lie naked and open:
the petrified eye staring up into the sky

a bleak view of what is still alive
of what invalidates itself

the mouth half open and prematurely assailed
has just laid the first letter

silence releases no scream

polar snow: myriads of weapons hang glistening
in the sun

(translated by Theo Hermans)

GOLDRUSH

I

A mangy god is stoking this fire
& the pockmarked rabble reveals the betrayal
like a bible of mud & moor

a greasy web of yellow-white sores envelops the skin
inhabitants chew on leather
a syphilitic ruff is more coveted
due to imposed respect for the wolfhound
& moorish caciques on their white stags

II

Quetzalcóatl's sun burns empty
miscarriage brackish water;
& rains encircle the lake

then tlaxcala swarm out
protected by a few harquebuses
& clamoring in countless boats
the city shrinks, a twitching sacrifice
crater of night-black hunger & wailing children

III

& now for a description of old customs:
trenches were filled with priests & cold nobility
the gates occupied by somewhat lesser gods
warriors slithered down the temple steps
coated with blood: slapstick of screaming animals
the palace of the sun was a slaughterhouse

hernán wrote his king, "& then to think that this race
is so barbarous, & so far removed from the knowledge of
    god"

IV
They tore open the women's skirts
hands searched everywhere
for gold, in their ears & hair & crazed
with lust men clutched at their breasts
sweating fingers groped at armpits along the flanks
& thighs of young girls

the guard of the black house was
thrown to the dogs

V
(malintzin)
There, in coyoacan, she sprawls
in the grass. this is
no accident: her fleshy
genius is scheming / like a sea
she spreads savage, capricious rancor,
a peaceful languor but behind salomé's mask
her beseeching mouth thrusts like a beak

pizotzin of culhuacan was also hanged

VI
Yellow corpses of women lie by the road
bodies ripe as maize, strangulated throats

xochipilli stuns the flowers gray
     —3 wise men came alone
     carrying their sheaves of bark
     there were 4, only 1 escaped
     the other 3 were seized,
     there in coyoacan—

VII
"We came together in amáxac
we had no more shields

we had no more macanas
we had no food no shelter
and it rained the whole night"

(manuscríto anónimo de tlatelolco)

(translated by Wanda Boeke)

THE HARTLAUB GULL

For Breyten Breytenbach, who is doing nine years in the cooler

A dream vision, Breyten, the print
of the bay
        you were mailing
as I went up in smoke
      of pipe tobacco and jet engines
          beyond
              over the empty sea—

the table full of maps and dates
no shelter, no sunshield,
         wine in the shadow
           of dusty shrubs;
color haze behind us—all
so distant
        that the island kept escaping the lens.

There and then are now
preserved;
        eternal present
is a slide show on the wall:

on the left a killer, hat
              over gutted eyes,
on the right a pimp
              with the sidelong glance of a truant

your one hand is caught
        in flight above the table top,
the other meets unseen
        with soft resistance of
              a neck or thigh or ovenwarm lap—

silently, attentively
we are on show

(is that the blur of the beloved's
hair fanning the edge?)

•

Boland close and the slammer
                far off as yet
we saw a white ant
run from Windhoek to Verneukpan
where a sweet fruit
        was mummified by the sun.

The man, that time, on the beach
with a gull on his head,
a monkey fled from your sketchpad;
              the wind
carried the fragrance
of women and birddung, seaweed and tar—

Yet,
as Cook did on his voyages
I see that island again,
          a place

where it is better to be a gull
than a human being

James C
4/27/1775

As we sailed from Table Bay we ob-
served Robben Island, a barren, sandy
place where many murderers and other
felons are held prisoner by the Dutch
East Indies Company, though there are
also some poor unfortunates among
them. Victims of the merciless tyr-
anny of these same merchants. Suffice
it to mention the King of Madura who,
robbed of his possessions and driven to
the utmost despair, there lives a hard
and miserable life in the despicable state
of a common slave.

Certainly, a sandy
place, where two centuries
later another visitor
slightly shifted the point of view

Most of all (he writes) I enjoyed
a camp on Robben Island in Table Bay

The island—no larger than Ellis Island—
is occupied by a small military garrison

Owing to the great hospitality and helpful-
ness
of the commander, Major Anderson,
we could camp
undisturbed
several hundred yards from the gull colony

Our main attention was directed
towards the aggressive behavior

shown by these birds in defending
their territory from their neighbors

The ten days on Robben Island flew by—
and consequently there was little time for
        more
than this cursory survey

Nevertheless
(Niko T adds)
nevertheless
we were not dissatisfied.

        •

Says the truant
who blows neither hot nor cold,

            —another bullshit artist I suppose,
another versifier measuring by two standards
in the land of Cockaigne;

while I'm pimping I'll take
            no smooth talker,
so whoever, at this place, here
passes the apposite fart
gets one, square on the mouth, free and for nothing.

The travesty, my friend, after the tragedy—

(translated by Greta Kilburn)

On Breyten Breytenbach, see the note on page 43. Niko T is the Anglo-Dutch natu-
ralist Niko Tinbergen.—Editors' Note.

Jacques Hamelink
(1939–   )

___

THE PYRENEES

I
Spirits of the Heights, I must face up to you.
There is baggage room left in my head
a wind lagoon I never used anyway.

Settle there. Expanse and distance
for as far as the eye can command: be within.
You come in handy
when I again thin to sheet of paper
or like winter crumple to a damask
tablecloth.

Mountain father, lodge in me
as I in you
with no return. This says

your servant, who cannot stand in your shadow,
cartoon character who in stopping
steals pebbles from you, snaps your picture,
briefly pisses in your melting snow, agape

at the length of breath with which you instruct
your rock gravel, your cumuli.

.   .   .

6
The laborers who belong
to the mountains are impassive,
take no notice of us,
daytrippers,
barely armored.

They represent
other worlds,
where we do not penetrate.

Difference of refraction.

Their chronometers are alpine,
geological, running on a quartz crystal.

They speak in past-tense stone tongue
to the profiles of condors
near the peaks.

We do not understand each other's
chronologies.

(translated by Scott Rollins)

STONETALK

You must move the speckled stone, the dead-tired stone
out of the wind, softly tease it out of
the swathings, warm it, cold stone, dear
stone, whisper sweet words, rock it,
until it feels less heavy, less immobile,
you must give the silent stone of your mouth
to play with,

you must take away the stone's heaviness,
you must take over the heaviness from the stone,
the stone at your breast, the stone in your lap has to
become lighter, more weightless, more floating,
luminous translucent body of redeemedness,
warm pulsing shell of a saint apparently dead,
you must provide the stone with last words
so that it can be freed entirely from matter,

and you must take its grayness upon yourself,
more and more, more completely all the time,
learn its lightness,
make silent your weak words, repent, endure
hardening until you can't feel a thing any more,
filled with nothing but the compact meaning of your mate-
    rial,
cool off until you drop below zero and time,
not even aware of the wind around you,
perfectly turned into heaviness,
in order that you may, sometime,
release from within yourself one
self-singing, solid, megalithic poem.

(translated by Ria Leigh-Loohuizen)

FOR THE SHADOW

They said reality was all there was
and that it demanded a choice.
You knew better, hesitant shadow.
You knew all along how the world
can shrink into the socket of an eye.
You knew that massive objects are empty
and how much stillness supports movement.

From you I learned that for some wings there
is no difference between solid and gaseous.
You were the only Chinese. Like a reed
you sometimes bent, amid a crowd, before a river.
For you I may have been no more than a cover
but there was no reality save through you.

(translated by Paul Vincent)

THE AMMONITE

instead of an apologia

Don't expect me to believe
that I'm one of the few
that can jump over his shadow.
The poles still have plenty of spring
but the team has lost some of its bounce
and a civilization's last takeoff
is bound to fail. I found this
for when the migration of the rocks erases us.
The rest's precarious. Plenty of
eras have come to an end
and what's hurricane force, what's a snail's pace?
What can one measure an ice cap with
but a man's expectation?
Plenty of houses, seemingly of basalt,
have been ablaze. Our time was never
the time of the ammonite
lying like a watch in the hand
but our time ticked in it too and it sang
like a Steinway, like a xylophone of mammoth bones.
Perhaps we won't make the other side,
perhaps the balsa raft will be waterlogged,

perhaps the soft tough twine won't hold.
Maybe we'll get separated.
Only if we endure will we see each other again,
beyond the rising tide of rocks.
Accept this hope, hollowest of forms,
as a rule of thumb. This round weather-hardened mineral,
found in the mountains, I hold tight for you,
onyx droplet of a world turned molten
so as to pass through the funnel;
this is the talisman
by which we'll know each other.
It contains all I have, my pride and my unrest.
I demand nothing, I am not ashamed.
Man was not an invention,
the relief in the rock not a sham.

(translated by Paul Vincent)

Hanny Michaelis
(1922–   )

WE CARRY EGGSHELLS . . .

We carry eggshells filled
to the brim with tears
carefully through time.

In the mirrors of our eyes
the world rises inhospitably.
We have been everywhere.
We return nowhere.

Laden with memories
we stoop towards the earth.
Ignorant and unwise
we wither away from the light
without a trace.

(translated by Marjolijn de Jager)

INVOLUNTARILY . . .

Involuntarily, almost
without noticing it
I have incorporated you
in the music which doesn't move you,
in the language which you don't speak
and don't understand, in me
whom you don't love.

(translated by Manfred Wolf)

THE ALARM'S CALLOUS RACKET

The alarm's callous racket
rips me from the warm cocoon
of sheets and blankets.

Dimly familiar
clothes on a chair
make the room
amazingly livable.

I turn around and
a naked man appears
on the edge of my bed.
I watch him smile
and I think
the woman who lives here
doesn't know what she's missing.

(translated by André Lefevere)

THREE FLIGHTS UP

Three flights up in Amsterdam's
inner city I think back
to the Rock of Gibraltar,
a sparkling pincushion
lifted up by the sea
toward low-hanging stars
while I thought back
to the picture of a hump
which stuck out of a blue plain,
often studied by a child
full of vague thoughts of later
which now is earlier.

(translated by Manfred Wolf)

IRREDEEMABLY BURIED . . .

Irredeemably buried
with the sand of two summers,
with three winters' snow.

But when I saw a picture in the news
of an assassinated guerrilla
in South America, who lay back
with half-closed eyes, oddly relaxed,
his unflawed torso naked to the waist
under his loosened shirt,
I felt something shift inside me
as if another body within my own
suddenly moved, opened its eyes,
then slowly closed them.

(translated by Marjolijn de Jager)

THE BODY . . .

The body
which takes satisfaction
in another body
since the one
became inaccessible
must from time to time
allow tacitly
that the mind
escape to a half
overgrown corner
of the memory,
and so betrays
treason itself.

(translated by Manfred Wolf)

BRILLIANTLY SPECULATING . . .

Brilliantly speculating
about life I let
the potatoes burn.
Undeniable proof
of emancipation.

(translated by James S Holmes)

SOMEWHERE IN THE HOUSE . . .

Somewhere in the house
a door slams shut
and a small giraffe
of bright orange plastic
totters briefly.
A present from a six-year-old
boy who, commuting
between bewildered parents,
bears his fate with
incomprehensible joy.

(translated by Marjolijn de Jager)

Hans Verhagen
(1939–   )

HANS VERHAGEN & SON

It was in the years 39,
the beginning of our era

●

Grows
(1st tooth
1st word
1st 2nd world war)
from one fairy tale
into the next one, step by step from childhood to a real hood
(or gun)
        ,Hans Verhagen

●

Began
well nourished,
300 calories extra under mother's petticoat

Began
blond, a poster (the sunny East)
, it was a good people year

(makes a good army)

(Every good mother a soldier's mother)

•

1
Grows bigger & bigger, more efficient than ever
in its big, organic
1-ness

2
Waken passions in a glove, that
turns a handle, that

•

Learns to tell time on a speedometer

And not till 20,000 miles unheard-of
perversities:

Remember?

Dressed only in top boots, socks,
shoes, slippers, nylons 9½—
soup eyes, a mouthful of drivel, but no morphine:

(Touched; slowly):

Love
——— etc.
Poetry

•

A human, hormones co-responsible,
7th armored division
not ruins, but new construction
expropriating,
appropriating
other people's
with-or-without-antisemitism
socialism

●

In our socialism there is no place
for socialists
: our program is restricted
to breathing.

In our poetry no breathing.
●

The human in his building,
subject to pigment,
although colorfast, i.e.
with humane traits—

And behind every wall
another wall, for
behind every wall is
another wall—
●

People.

Treading the 1st sq. ft. of emotion under thought
as under foot they try
their footwear, towards a fine time coming

Maneuvering people, avoiding
each other, embracing,
escaping

People.
●

These people never check their movements or
the motives for their movements
: these people move

And that is all there is to be said
of what they said,
but they said nothing

•

The human dominates in the human,
the human needs cod-liver oil
particularly in winter

•

Spelling out formulas in the genitals
according to the scenario of love

,

last winter pelleted with impulses
as in every psychiatric clinic

:

philosophies of life made to order,
in a toddler by the atmosphere

–

a new industry in poetry

!

•

A fine time for the
aerial photographers.
Caterpillar tracks
encircle the world

The system's not good,
is not bad, is the
system. Caterpillar tracks
round & round & round &

A fine time in which
my heart beats like an
aerial photographer's
heart; the caterpillar tracks

•

Unheard because of the caterpillars
is the stealing
of my overcoat,
stolen in a stolen
attaché case.

And coming home in a new coat—
                , Norman Verhagen

•

It was in the years 61,
the beginning of our era

                        (translated by James S Holmes)

CANCER

A painless lump
could be more ominous
than a painful one.

•

Normally,
all parts of the body grow to a certain point
and then stop—

The nose does not continue to grow indefinitely.

Imagine, then,
that suddenly one part begins to grow beyond
its normal limits.

For no apparent reason.

•

He offered me a cigar,
and I declined it.

I said, "If I told you
that smoking would give
you a cancer of the mouth
would you stop smoking?"

"No," he replied.

•

Aid only is not sufficient;
confidence and faith in recovery alone
have no influence at all.

Even if 99% of all cancer cells
have been removed or destroyed—

then the remaining 1% will kill the patient.

•

Now ask yourself this question:

"Have I any roughened, warty patches
on my skin; or any ulcerated areas?"

If the answer is "yes,"
then ask yourself if it is cancer.

Don't die of cancer,
you can live.

•

A moment later, though, I noticed
that you weren't breathing at all.

The post-mortem examination showed
a tumor composed of immature cells.

The metastatic spread was found in
many sites, including unusual ones.

There were ulcers in the stomach:
No wonder you had convulsions.

The miracle is that you could live
in such a broken-down house so long.

(translated by the author and Peter Nijmeijer)

STARS

World where no nightingale can sing.

Wallpaper
painted with yellowed
faded roses.

World, cruel
sometimes.

A. slowly rising.
•

Fridge, washing machine, television.

B. blooms sideways and explodes.

Glittering fireworks, sparks, stars,
crackling, hissing, extinguishing again.

•

And 1, 2, 3;
bang, bang, bang,
C. *shoots* upwards.

(translated by Peter Nijmeijer)

Fritzi Harmsen van Beek
(1927–   )

INTRODUCTION TO A PRAYER

One day when the sun shone on the water and Golden-
march found the cuckoo's young in her bed

more lovable than dandelions, stronger than chick-
like mimosa feathers (or probably the opposite)

and called him Dog's Frog for, naked, red and with
the grim face of dependency on love was he. And:

—Little father, little father, may I keep him?—No child,
you must return him to the King of Life and Death.

And Death, so she took a long knife and butchered the old
neck in the late hour, to let the blood drain off

with the sunset. So she did. And her young in a basin by
the window to let it grow like a cabbage. Hey, dollikin,

then the tables grew crooked, the mirrors blurred and
money still scarcer. And when his small voice

wept: Eat heartily, she sat with wolves and magicians
deep in the gardens, or worse, high on the roof, trans-

parent with wellbeing but too torn and too badly informed
to see the spoon in their beaks, as amorous

as a waiter and much more obsequious. Bad service was
often the complaint, but ah well, pom pom pom. So she got

a beating on her behind with a bunch of plastic flowers
bought with money from his piggybank and he asked for a
    reckoning!

Well, she said: Think of me as of that cat, whose penance
you wrote out for her because she couldn't write herself:

"Mothers may not eat mice, enchanted rabbits,
princes or dragons. Dieu des Enfants, may they fast

and pray, amen." Repeat a thousand times.

                    (translated by Claire Nicolas White)

GOOD MORNING? HEAVENLY MADAM PING

*(To my despondent cat, by way of consolation on the demise of her
litters)*

did the gentle night agree with you, did the mis
chievous, secretive plants duly give forth

fragrance and did none hopefully of your remaining
infants succomb to the bubonic plague?

Have you examined the interesting jittery
religious birds yet, pious benevolent

Madam, phoning back and forth their: this is tweet,
come and sit on my bough—oh the graceful

vivacious birds, all all prey to good puss,
the sorely tried sad mother. Damn it all,

this disease, dear unfortunate Madam,
is a cruel rascal and this much is clear:

you can't outrival it with childbearing, where even the
undertaker, that intimate companion, that

very familiar provider, also, of lukewarm milk,
on its extended hind legs can hardly

keep pace any more with committing to
earth, isn't that right, Lady Ping, radar-whiskered

double-wimpled, madam-eyed grimalkin?
It would be better now to sit without sad longing in

the raw fragrant morning air, now that the sun is
still tender and the curtains lively in the good

merry wind. Oh flag-tailed excellent person,
look, reticent imbecile dearest of all,

there's an arresting, very tiny but particularly
tasty creature walking between the pebbles

underneath the sky-blue hydrangea

(translated by Greta Kilburn)

Riekus Waskowsky
(1932–1977)

SALT PEANUTS

When I woke up this morning, I thought,
thought ear-splittingly:
Salt Peanuts! Salt Peanuts!
It was really a remarkable experience
bordering on satori.
Salt Peanuts! Salt Peanuts!

Kant for example—Mein lieber Herr Immanuel Kant—
would never have done such a thing
(an early morning in the universe
and a damn cold one too).
He was a nice old scarecrow
people could set their clocks by.
Salt Peanuts! Salt Peanuts!

Pretty dangerous, that! All those sextons
of Königsberg hanging out of their towers
to set their clocks by Kant.
Hundreds plunged to their deaths,
tumbling from the categorical imperative
onto their bare backsides.
Salt Peanuts! Salt Peanuts!

En summa, meine Herrschaften, when I woke up
this morning,
Salt Peanuts! Salt Peanuts!
my bed smelled of a young girl,
of our lies large and small,
of a single moment of understanding,
one moment out of eternity
while the universe and my neighbor behind the thin wall
held their breaths and possibly choked to death.
Salt Peanuts! Salt Peanuts!

And I thought what a good thing it was the King
later declared it strictly forbidden
to set clocks by Kant.
Salt Peanuts! Salt Peanuts!

(translated by James S Holmes)

ESSAY

They had warned him so often: "Play it
cool, Orestes! All those obscure complexes
of your sister's are really not worth a destiny."

He wouldn't listen. He sullenly stared
at Electra and the sunny hills of Argos.
All he could see was the marble bathroom far off
where Blodeuwedd and Gronw had done in his
father after an ancient manner (a mid-
summer nightmare).

He rushed inside and took his own blood
mother with his sword.

(translated by James S Holmes)

"Agamemnon dies in a peculiar manner: with a net thrown over his head, with one
foot still in the bath, but the other on the floor, and in the bath-house annexe . . . a
situation recalling the midsummer death in Mabinogion of the sacred king Llew Llaw,
at the hands of his treacherous wife Blodeuwedd and her lover Gronw (Wales)." Rob-
ert Graves, *The Greek Myths*.—Author's Note.

IF BY ETERNITY

*If by eternity is understood not endless temporal duration but time-
lessness, then he lives eternally who lives in the present.*—WITTGEN-
STEIN, *Tractatus* 6.4311

Read through another chapter of Ludwig's
last night—cf. supra—and phoned B. at once.

Yes, she said, and for eternity I thought
I'd give the good emperor Huang Ti's
old and trusted method (2698 BC) a try.

Gandalf 13: "Gnashing his teeth and heaving
deep sighs he pressed the semen mixed
with woman's moisture back to the brain;
he grew so old that people later
could not remember whether he had died at all."

B. came and there was a lot of eternity between her thighs
but now as she's getting up to look for a cigarette
I notice I'm a mere mortal after all. Pale drops

drip on my dark floor. I hear them ticking
like a far-off clock.

(translated by André Lefevere)

THAT THE SUN WILL RISE TOMORROW

That the sun will rise tomorrow is a hypothesis.—WITTGENSTEIN,
Tractatus 6.36311

Still I do think he's losing
his grip . . . I mean of course Him:
on a rainy day in eternity
thinking up some universe, some
earth & people & time . . .

So here we are: God's private
thoughts in an odd moment—naturally
it adds up to a history of
blood, sweat, & tears . . .

Tired of it all we wait
for the roll of thunder calling Him
inside: "Come along son,
wash your hands & blow your nose—
the Messiah is on the way . . . "

(translated by the author)

Hans Faverey
(1933–   )

STARING AT AN EMPTY SPACE

Staring at an empty space
kills more than all the centuries
of smoke blown out
by the mountain coming after.

As long as the delusion reigned,

I pursued the bitter
chimera deep into the
newly opening land.

The first swallow of this spring
had to get rid of all
the meanings I never want to
find again even in my sleep.

(translated by J. M. Coetzee)

FIRST THE MESSAGE KILLS

First the message kills
the receiver, then
it kills the sender.
It does not matter
in what language.

I get up, push
the French windows open
and breathe.

I am not going to lure
the gulls circling
above the street empty of snow by
making feeding motions.

I light a cigarette;
return to my post,
and breathe.

It is not a question of dreaming.
Anything is possible.
It doesn't make that much difference.

                    (translated by J. M. Coetzee)

CHRYSANTHEMUMS, ROWERS

I
The chrysanthemums
that stand in the vase on the table
by the window: these

are not the chrysanthemums
that stand by the window
on the table
in the vase.

The wind that annoys you
and ruffles your hair

is the wind that ruffles your hair;
it is the wind that you don't any
longer want to be annoyed by
when your hair is ruffled.

2
Only when someone in the photo
stands out large as life
waiting for his death
is he recognized.

They all stand on the brink
looking at their own
birdie; on the point of laughing: all of them.

No one recognizes himself in this photo.
What is there "sudden" in a mirror?
Mirrors never recognize anyone.
What is there "sudden" in a photo?

Making out a hand
before my eyes, I hope for all I'm worth
that it is a hand of my own,
or that it is a hand
that would like to belong with me.

3
If I want to go and do something
then I must already have got up
to want to go and do it;
or I must have wanted it

already done: to be able
to get up in such a way that I

would have to do it;

and in the process having
lost the way,
did as it wanted
itself done, with no hard feelings:
although nothing had happened.

and I did not want to be absent,
because that way I did not know myself,
when it was about to happen.

4
Insofar as it brings about something
and has forgotten itself,
it is vain
and in god's name.

The utter void
in each thing, which is
real, and as such active,
which mingles with the echo
of the last word:

(that no longer wishes to pass
the lips), which at first still caresses

those lips, then without qualm
attacks them—this hopeless lack
that everywhere makes knots in water
and is a needle in bread.

5
Gradually; that is how
they approach: 8 rowers,
ever farther inland

growing in their mythology:
with each stroke ever farther
from home, rowing with all their might,
growing till there is no more water
and they fill the whole landscape

to the brim. Eight—
rowing ever farther
inland; landscape where by now there is no
more water—overgrown
landscape by now. Landscape,
rowing ever farther in-

land; land
without rowers; land by now over-
rown.

(translated by J. M. Coetzee)

THE SEVENTIES:
NEO-REALITY AND
A RETURN TO FORM

Taking away,
writing is
taking away . . .
　—ROLAND JOORIS, "Writing"

. . . I
like a group of words that
suddenly start feeling really close
to each other & say: let's stay together
forever, we don't need anybody else.
　—HERMAN DE CONINCK, "Ars Poetica: 4"

A word turns image, a bikeride turns emotion.
　—AD ZUIDERENT, "Return to Solitude"

. . . my mental
Bent is to muscles bound, more than bound verse.
　—GERRIT KOMRIJ, "The Woman in the Arts"

In the tearoom sits the poet and
stirs the lukewarm pot of emotions round
and round.
　—HANS VLEK, "Famine Winter"

. . . what was I for god's sake supposed to do with the truth?
　—HANS TENTIJE, "Icarian Is the Sea"

Patrick Conrad
(1945–   )

ZEPPELINS

Dans la souffrance physique au moins nous n'avons pas à choisir nous-
mêmes notre douleur.—MARCEL PROUST

Wednesday night, in the zeppelin:
—"Oh, Look!"
—"It's the moon gliding under our thighs!"
—"Ici, nous sommes seules."
—"Yes Pierre, this is a fine place."

There are moths in the fin-de-siècle fur and time
and again, really time and again she says "feel this," she
       moans
she says "feel this," and Pierre moans.

She, she's called Margaret, she, she Pierre.

Like the hard light-green peony
that tries to develop quite hardly slender
her nails rasp seeking through the zone.

Their laughter:
tender as only when two women
slide and rustle triangle to triangle through time
the expedition of teeth that land behind lips.

Their tears:
troubled as only when two women in love
tattoo to tooth the nipple
to waist the tongue.

On the paper wall with the arum lilies faded
a unique photograph:
"First application of Electricity to Aeronautics:
Nacelle and Siemens Motor for the Dirigible
made by the Tissandier brothers
Albert (left) and Gaston (right), 1883–1884."

And underneath in the deep divan conjoined
with Margaret animally Pierre through the broad purple
     wedge
and across the porch the day comes tumbling in like plush.

Pull the Turkish not the Egyptian ring from your forefinger
perhaps because of the wound.
(Margaret had already silently turned to water.)
Melancholy is being alone though together with
beyond the balcony the room ammoniac
and the bed like a well.

Margaret sees in her eyes the whole room clammy
with the plaster and the decanters convex
and the peace and the order that reign
in the works of the clock.

But just as the moon fades with the hours
and then disappears
your eyes too will wilt like two droplets
hesitant first then suddenly.

No bronzed but an opaline pit your ass
your thighs a face late in the morning tomorrow

you will ascend with me to oil the motor
in the stars Pierre.

Yes.

(translated by James S Holmes)

ROXY'S

Madam, wearing a wig, has the calm jaws of a cow.
And out of Five-Dollar Billy's bosom
creeps gnawing a plaster squirrel.

And though the Wurlitzer's sound isn't 100%
its light is the finest light
and the warmest ever to flow over Zoë
and the other mild girls.

9:20 P.M.
The sweat of paying customers shines on Fifi's despairingly
    narrow pelvis.
Or is it paint?

I'll say it again:
Or is it paint?

But in her cunt, everyway, closed
and flat as the palm of an open hand,
ticks a clock, right-angled and admonitory:

"There is so much good in the worst of us,
And so much bad in the best of us,
That it little behooves any of us,
To talk about the rest of us."

And today, precisely today and like every day,
begins the first night of the rest of your life.
And I see: you're weeping so hard
the tears run along your thighs.

The brothel atrophies to museum:
The Liberty Bell splits, the carpets sour,
the Psenner-Pauff calendar turns to stone.
This is a timeless dreary theater,
still as a still life and cruel as woman.

Oh! Conscious tenderness!
Oh! Kitsch! Oh! Camp!

Oh my love, Miss Cherry Delight!
Keep your sister's letters hidden away
for all this evil and pain
and fucking generals. I'll come and see you
one of these days. Hold on Cherry and cry
if you need to.

Tenderly,

P.

(translated by Peter Nijmeijer)

This and the two following poems are from Conrad's *11 Sad Songs for Edward Kienholz 1970–1971;* the titles are those of works by the painter Kienholz.—Editors' Note.

THE ILLEGAL OPERATION

She, the mother, the sow, the soft sac,
caught hold of the lamp in despair
with four red, contagious fingers
like bodkins.

And out of the burlap hollow flows warm mud,
the scarlet worm, the fragrant cake.

She, the mother, the fertilized triangle, the accused,
throws up the blind honey of her belly,
the superfluous timid food.

And in the bowl beside the chair, the tongs and scissors
tame the monster in the slanting shadow.
What still filters in this tiny kitchen
is the delicious nostalgia and some spittle.

She, the mother, the barmaid, the womb,
wrenches the wreck in revenge
from her musty flesh.

But he who's permitted to die before
his birth attains the sole and genuine form
of immortality.

(translated by Peter Nijmeijer)

THE BACK SEAT DODGE '38

This is an accidental couple like millions
with their heads fused; bits of woman
under a man of air
and on the radio: Hawaii.

Safely under this thin rusty roof
his gentle claw, his porphyry paw
whispers sweet nothings to her weeping slit.

Such as sea, war, cub and compassion.

And in heaven upside down she sees the tops of the beeches
breaking as if trembling in the water of a pond.

If I had to call them by their names,
I'd call them:
you and I.

And the smell was the smell
of rain and rain
on grass.

(translated by Peter Nijmeijer)

Roland Jooris
(1936–   )

SOMEWHAT MINIMAL

a cube
i.e. a box,
an emptiness or
a thought
packed visibly
in its dimensions;

but also
a thing in space
even if it's
simply a piece of it
a sporty occupant;

a cube: I set my
beer on it.

(translated by James S Holmes)

MINIMAL

Bird bobs.
Branch creaks.
Sky clouds up.

Almost nothing
to look at
and just that
I observe.

(translated by Peter Nijmeijer)

VILLAGE

a village is a circle
drawn by hand
around a church;

a dove is a very
simple line void of air
on a rooftop;

a spring season leaves wet
stains on the paper
of the sky;

and look, now this is true
reality: I shall presently
let it rain
on my poem
so that it runs
into a watercolor
of sodden,
illegible words.

(translated by Theo Hermans)

DENSITY

Mist. Say
nothing now.
Much is left unsaid.
A little is much.
The word hardly
hardly moves
in the wind
which is nowhere.

Say nothing now.
Wipe out nothing.
On the same surface
of night. Against which
scarcely and nowhere.

(translated by Peter Nijmeijer)

CUCKOO

Like a cuckoo
I should like to
call now and again,
hidden somewhere
in a grove
on the edge
of farmland;

like a cuckoo
I should like
each year anew
with my solitary
fragment of text
to be a perfectly

natural part
of the summer,
present yet
nowhere to be found
in my language
estate.

(translated by Theo Hermans)

WRITING

Taking away,
writing is
taking away,

so that
all I leave
is a flowerpot
standing brick red
on the windowsill
and watch twilight
fill in a corner
of the room
with pencil.

(translated by Peter Nijmeijer)

Eddy van Vliet
(1942–   )

BIRTH

if something should go wrong
—but this is unlikely—
the deposit on the cradle will be refunded

the expense of printing
"we're proud to announce"
however remains due

•

when she gasped for breath
with a tongue whiter
than my dinner jacket
and her eyes rolled
where an orgasm would never have put them

the number of chromosomes was irrevocably determined

•

from birth onward
the child's sense of hearing declines

the room is filled with flowers
the first six weeks the child is blind.

                    (translated by Peter Nijmeijer)

IN THESE EXHAUSTING LOWLANDS

In these exhausting lowlands
where coldness is a habit
and the sun a recollection
of what spring basely forecasts

she's waiting
for the window to expose her breath
for the sadness round her aging body
to kiss the mirrors to a haze of grief

words are not her speech
with the patience of the hamster
she weaves signs together

to the imaginary lovers it is
but a confusing book of gestures
an invitation more gentle than the word
to the Initiated.

(translated by Peter Nijmeijer)

STOCKHOLM

You smell of Amsterdam, but there's an end to it.
Your glasses saw it all too big,
if marble steps and gold leaf
betoken history
and history is complacency.

Conversing about coal and steel
you danced through two world wars
in the Royal Winter Garden of the Grand Hotel,
a bearskin cap full of smiles
at Svenska Handelsbanken.

A ship wrecked in sight of fame
does you credit now, as does
in one of your rare bars a drunken actor who
sick to death of your crowns
wanted to take his own life.

Why of all places did it have to be in your streets
that I read how Robert Lowell
coming from Kennedy Airport
took his last cab?

(translated by Theo Hermans)

From AFTER THE LAWS OF GOOD-BYE & AUTUMN

Every soldier in the streetcar was a relation
a hand in my hair
a handful of chocolate

My mother's gentleness
was fixed in photographs
saved up in cardboard boxes
dying amongst corned beef at the Rhine
or pinned up in a truck
driving from Milwaukee to LA

The wonders of the world
spilled over me like confetti
a banana, an orange, a Negro,
Glenn Miller and a Jew in the street.
•

I was shown snapshots to prove
I could have been nobility
if one fine day my father
hadn't come biking into the house

And as straightforward as always
won the young girl
with languages he didn't know
above a second-hand violin
he attributed to Guarneri

Consoling me he could make
neckties out of old dresses
trimmed my hair on Sundays
& had the strongest toes I knew

I slept on faded photo albums
full of native boys, white palaces and
parasols to a background of racehorses.

•

A bright-yellow sweater on a sheet of grass
so I lay, tempting and thirteen years old
peeping at long-skirted girl's-model bikes
from between a locust's legs

My dagger partitioned countries in the sand
laying waste what I could
the corn and the wheat,
creeping along canals I led
crusades of hate against the farmers

O what heroes we were
a handkerchief full of life poured out
at night beneath the lash
of cruel princesses.

(translated by James S Holmes)

THE SHORELINE DOESN'T CHANGE

The shoreline doesn't change for the fisherman
who casts his nets each day
unaware of the pottery beneath the mud

The soil has always been soil to the farmer
pacing his field
over shark cemeteries

Granite is hard and eternal and so is marble
to the child that skims rocks
umpteen feet high eroded
to pebbles over the surface of the water

Time was infallibly precise
to the Maya priests who after 260 days
entered a new year

And yet I ask you sometimes
"when are you coming back?"
as tears on your cheeks evaporate in the air
and are mixed with the dust of a century to come.

(translated by Theo Hermans)

OLD CHAMPAGNE GLASS

A cloud no bigger than a button
drifts across your face

There you lie, a trifle matt,
a little depressed by the frosty air,
at the Sunday market among silver-plated spoons
and a chessboard without knights

The lipstick on your forehead is gone
the dreams have been settled

Without a date or emblem, neither beautiful
nor worn out, but simply old,
you're waiting for a buyer, but more still
for the fall of a bicycle bell right above your open mouth.

(translated by Theo Hermans)

GREEN. I REWRITE

Green. I rewrite. It turns greener.
Whereon the fields—like a command—
expand, look inward and
fall in the sensuousness of night.

An enameled pail. The red
attracted, so, attention.
A white pail filled with blood.

(translated by James S Holmes)

Mark Insingel
(1935–   )

THE GARDENS, BETRAYED

The gardens, betrayed
to the curious,
lock him up, lu–
natic of rooms.

The rooms, between
corridors and halls,
torture of foot–
steps and windows.

Between the glass, where
noises burst into
knives and in the
attendants' grins, a
peacock of shame.

(translated by James S Holmes)

DESCARTES

to be or not to be
that is the question

to question or not to question
that is to be

to be or not to be question
that is to question

to question or not to be
that is to be

(written in English)

WITH HEADS HELD HIGH

with heads held high
with heads held high and in straight lines
with heads held high and in straight lines and with banners
    waving
with heads held high and in straight lines and with banners
    waving and at a steady pace
with heads held high and in straight lines and with banners
    waving and at a steady pace and with songs resounding
with heads held high and in straight lines and with banners
    waving and at a steady pace and with songs resounding
    and in bright uniforms
with heads held high and in closed ranks and with banners
    waving and at a steady pace and with songs resounding
    and in bright uniforms

with heads held high and in closed ranks and following the
  flag and at a steady pace and with songs resounding and
  in bright uniforms
with heads held high and in closed ranks and following the
  flag and in march time and with songs resounding and in
  bright uniforms
with heads held high and in closed ranks and following the
  flag and in march time and with songs thundering and in
  bright uniforms
with heads held high and in closed ranks and following the
  flag and in march time and with songs thundering and in
  battle dress
with grinning faces and in closed ranks and following the flag
  and in march time and with songs thundering and in
  battle dress
with grinning faces and like a gang and following the flag
  and in march time and with songs thundering and in
  battle dress
with grinning faces and like a gang and pursuing the people
  and in march time and with songs thundering and in
  battle dress
with grinning faces and like a gang and pursuing the people
  and on the double and with songs thundering and in bat-
  tle dress
with grinning faces and like a gang and pursuing the people
  and on the double and roaring and shouting and in battle
  dress
with grinning faces and like a gang and pursuing the people
  and on the double and roaring and shouting and spat-
  tered with blood.

(translated by James S Holmes)

Herman de Coninck
(1944–   )

ARS POETICA: 4

for buddingh'

what I like is poems
like muscled men with hairy
mantalk, poems that scratch
where it itches, come up to you
oozing health & say: sit down,
I'm a poem, I'm pleased to
meet you & what shall we talk about.

poems like that of course can speak
about love as easily as about vietnam,
& maybe they are responsible
for poetry's health, the way
farmers in limburg are
for the health of morality.

but actually even more I
like a group of words that
suddenly start feeling really close
to each other & say: let's stay together
forever, we don't need anybody else.

(translated by James S Holmes)

On Limburg see the note on page 131.—Editors' Note.

FRÉDÉRIQUE, OR HOW I BECAME A HISTORIAN

december 20th 1965, the sun
blushes like a franciscan.
the river twists
through the land with bold thigh-thrusts
the way a sense of power moves through a king.
& I still love frédérique.
how I might know the secrets
of her body & call her breasts
breasts, as if I might call a celebrity
by his first name.
& sometimes I simply gave her
a slap on the ass.

how she could snuggle her un-
definedness against me till I defined it
in a kiss & she said:
frédérique, *enchantée,*
& she sunned herself in my sins & I
passed over her like four seasons & she took
place underneath me & became a world event
in my arms & made history, I have
become a historian.

(translated by James S Holmes)

EVERY DAY HERE IS LIKE THIS

every day here is like this: the flowers
growing beyond the palings, trees
blowing at 6s & 7s, & clarity
that streams in from everywhere
like fans for a soccer game.
the sun is already running on-
to the field, beaming confidence.

& the poets here are equally strong.
their firm images work reality
the way farmers work the land,
they can carry in their arms an entire
reality.

I love this land.
if I ever emigrate I'll take it with me.
I shall say its name
& it will follow me.

(translated by James S Holmes)

THE RHINOCEROS

he is as portly
as any self-important fool.
he is something like the twentieth century
before christ, suddenly standing up
in history and taking one little step
forward,
he really can't speed it up much.

he is made of flexible concrete,
as solemn as an apartment block collapsing
in slow motion when he
sits down, lies down,

to meditate in his inner being
which is as empty as a bunker
in which there have not been any
soldiers since '44.

(translated by Theo Hermans)

A BRITON

is someone who, walking into a department store,
is capable of knocking and asking:
"no inconvenience?"

maybe a briton is an inconvenience to himself,
a british temperament must be something like
a trestle bed, uncomfortable to sleep on.

but it does help one to acquire the discipline
to keep emotions at a distance,
the way one even keeps a cigarette at a distance
by means of (pronounce as english,
to keep french at a distance)
a porte-cigarette.

and it helps one to acquire the gentleman's hauteur.
I still believe that wellington, on seeing
napoleon's troops at waterloo, had
this comment: "quite interesting."

(translated by Theo Hermans)

MOTHER

What you do with time
is what an old grandmother clock
does with it: strikes twelve o'clock
& takes plenty of time doing it.
You are the clock: time passes
but you remain. You wait.

Waiting is what happens to a garden
underneath snow, a tree trunk
underneath moss, hope of better times coming
in the nineteenth century,
words in a poem.

Because poetry has a lot to do with letting
things grow moldy together,
turning grapes into alcohol,
making facts into jelly, mason-jar canning
of words, in the cellar of yourself.

(translated by James S Holmes)

H. H. ter Balkt
(1938–   )

THE ANIMALS' CRUSADE

One day the cages and caverns opened
Out came the cavebear the mammoth the seafaring
shag, cormorant in verse, the gray-headed vulture
the ram from the mountains, the dagger-wielding shark
From the look on their snouts you could tell they meant
    business
You could hear by their beating wings and their grumbling
They had shrugged off their humiliation, cast off their yoke
once laid upon them by that mysterious hero of an Adam
the one in his garden
In a word, they'd had it up to here
And the moral of the hunting rifle lay thrown off
the skinned fur of the flight faded
The adder walked erect and the boar wore polaroids
that lent him a pleasant look The beavers
gnawed down telephone poles and so broke off all commu-
    nication
At the head, which was to be expected, the black lion black
as black gold and gold-colored as pitch black
It was a magnificent procession, dazzling
At the rear, the unicorn reported missing, the dodo, the pas-
    senger pigeon
alongside the viruses and exuberant spermatozoa

Thus trod
the holy animals through the sacred world

And do you know how or why?
O no, they just wandered, they had no pope!
Sometimes they tore a man to shreds for joy
or milked a city dry
Crucified a Jesus every now and then
or felled a prophet or a prince
They never grew tired
No need to hurry
They had no commandments

(translated by Scott Rollins)

ELEGY OF THE HOGS

There is something so sad in the wise eyes of hogs
that makes them like prophets before the slaughter.
(I'm not too wild about prophets and you? No
I much prefer the vine of ivy climbing)
Their tusks yanked out as they slip out of nature's body
on the conveyor belt, exodus from blazing Egypt
through the red sea of their deliverance, headed for straw
and the knife-clustered idols of mankind.
Sometimes one, an old boar, stands under the ancient
tree of knowledge, ancient species of apple dying out
dead-still, looking at the wind on the horizon,
blinder by insight than by nature almost.

Almost you see, in the bridal veils of autumnal myrtle
in the lisping wind, in the spiciness, the thought-
balloon on its top-heavy head: Striped, I ran, wild boar

once, and what am I now! O pity those tamed
hogs, they are the poets amongst the animals,
melancholic and of little use until burnt down
against the wall, their layer of fat bursts open like an elegy.

(translated by Scott Rollins)

THE MILL

The mill that hangs open like a mouth
for the owls for brown owls and the wind
The door builds its groan on its hinge
Hours: like the wagons the clocks are gone

Gone is a distant land; creatures swing their searchlight
on the doorstep; field mice searching for old grain
The sail hangs still as a legendary sword
of the forgotten leader of a house short of sagas

Because the hand that in the motionless millstone
engraved the old saying: *Wind is the breath of time*
lettered in a chest in Usselo is calling for
deliverance, owl, you know that, owl? the wind says
"Nostalgia, plowman and digger, plows me under"

Spooky and hornlike the windowpane cocks its henfoot
and scratches on the primeval prospect of the moors
Nostalgia, sings the swallow, that holds me down . . .
The owl cocks the trigger of his eye in vain:
only the shadow of the mill and no mouse

(Holding a mouse is his best pose) Then
the dialogue falters when the tower-black night

climbs in the bushes and the hanging bat shivers
How big they are, the silent owl and the soundless wind
their gazes dressed for ending fixed on the smoldering city.

(translated by Scott Rollins)

Usselo is a village in the east of the Netherlands, not far from the German border.
—Editors' Note.

THE FOUND

The lost objects
signal in Morse, inaudible
Hundreds of found objects
sheltering in depots and police stations
filling the closets the worn-out shelves
with lostness no one comes to claim
It's nearly a miracle
there are other lost objects
never to be found;
you search for them in vain
among the found objects
The telephone rings and rings
in their sanatorium
The cities are full of lost objects
These are found by thieves
and some are not claimed,
since they are the wrong found things.

(translated by Scott Rollins)

Gerrit Komrij
(1944–   )

FERTILE

The nightingales grow out of my warm thighs
And sing sweet songs about the state of things.
Watching me make giant horny cow eyes,
You catch the tone of desolate mocking.

Anemones grew from Adonis' blood!
And he drank all of Lethe drained and dry.
Just to imagine that I ever should
Have to do it: No, that one I'll pass by.

Things mix in me as in a butterdish.
Someday I'll spin them to wild tragic tales!
You must do things like that. Or you're a dead fish.
So come to me and stroke my nightingales.

(translated by Jacob Lowland)

ON YOUR BACK

It is as if you're lugging a commode
On your back, such a day. Just stretch that back,
Drawer after drawer falls on the ground. Odd's blood,
your body's all over black-and-blue tracks.

Off you start again; you calmly pick up
The drawers and, hup, on your back—now that should
Stay put awhile—hell, oh go shove it up
The creek, there they all go again, for good.

It's too much. A while back you saw this guy
His chest to frontwards, like someone peddling
Door to door, but a wily one. On the sly
He'd glued it shut; you couldn't see a thing.

(translated by Jacob Lowland)

THE WOMAN IN THE ARTS

Madame *hates* men who with a look will gnash
And gnaw her and regardless spit her out.
She'd rather tarry there where her weak flesh
Is celebrated with a gallant pout

By moonsick arty types glad that she should
Wear her face where it is, not Back Behind.
She asks me whether I too think this world
Is not the real one? And do I not find

Hans' poems ("soft, sweet Hans!") Experimental
And Cosmic? I straightface the smile that curls

My lips: "Madame, Your Opposite: my mental
Bent is to muscles bound, more than bound verse."

(translated by Jacob Lowland)

"Soft, sweet Hans" is Hans Lodeizen (see pp. 26-32). "This world is not the real one"
is a well-known line from one of Lodeizen's poems.—Editors' Note.

AN AFTERNOON

You sat there frailly in your gold-stitched froc.
Waiting until he wheeled the teacart in.
Your friend sat next to you, spelling a book
(Sesame and Lilies), but now and then

Nodding, or staring in the draperies.
There was the tinkling sound of porcelain
In the kitchen, the place assigned as his,
Where he had to find his way on a chain.

Your friend set up the Chinese checker board.
You rang for tea (if only, you were thinking,
He hadn't jumped me then, like a wild boar)
And he came in the room, rattling and clanking.

(translated by Jacob Lowland)

THE HOMECOMING

The maid was thoroughly drilled. Work and slave
Round the clock, she would. A real jewel.
Everything gleamed. Sure this was not a flash

In the pan, they had no qualms to leave
Hearth and home in her hands, when for a whole
Year they went off to live abroad. Fresh

Back, what a fearsome scene; they were appalled.
It cut like a razor across the flesh.
It made a ruckus. It was not to be believed.

(translated by Jacob Lowland)

THE DRAGONS

His coffin, lined top, sides, and back
With scarlet velvet, seesaws down the drive
Drawn by two dragons, neck and flanks draped black.
And there he lies now, packaged for the grave.

He was a Writer. Even Writers die.
It's cruel but true. Out of the question that
His pen will pour forth more of all that high
Beauty. He lies too stiff beneath the sheet.

Now he's drawn along by his favorite
Dragons, Big Eleanor and Little Rose.
The smaller one of his Creative Art,
The other, larger one of his Elbows.

(translated by Jacob Lowland)

THE UNICORN

The unicorn strides in its house of glass
Towards the flamingo, quivering snow white.

The bird knows: now something will come to pass.
Then the unicorn stabs. There is no cry.

But through the cupola there sounds the *pffft*
Of blood that leaks and rustles from the flank
Of the flamingo, turning gray as grit
As it dies with a soft, disarming squawk.

The unicorn, after it's drunk the blood,
Rises in rapture, then with all its might
Shudders, turns color, is transmogrified
Into a peacock-blue hermaphrodite.

(translated by Jacob Lowland)

THE COMREIGH CRITTER

A fabled beast there is that's called Comreigh,
A strangish name for something that's so pleasing.
It's true its head is just as broad as high,
But otherwise it won't make you uneasy.

He's slightly rattlebrained, a kind of flop.
His hands are very like to two coal shovels.
The head is where it should be though, on top.
He'll never blossom into something lovely.

He's basically a dog. All his lifetime
He'll be a beast that "always understands."
Only deep in the night he sometimes whines,
Half stifled by a hurt from unseen hands.

(translated by Jacob Lowland)

Jan Kuijper
(1947–   )

BULLRUSH BASKET

There are no crocodiles or hippos here.
Giant leaves reach down to the shore beneath.
Great lilies poke their stamens from the sheath.
The river flows, slow and brown and unclear.
I'm not afraid of some fierce animal.
I don't belong here. Strangers don't get hurt.
My eyelids make me inviolable.
Through a chink I see a different world.

Different yet the same. Here too it's warm.
And dark besides: the draperies are shut.
Did something move? What kind of ticking's that?
I feel four eyes: all four are focused on
me. I want out, hide my face in my arm,
wooden Behemoth, tin Leviathan.

(translated by Jacob Lowland)

STARCHART

A naked woman chained against a cliff.
I didn't know who by. A whale swam near.
Only a small one, but she looked as if
there must be danger, and it threatened her.
A tired-looking kid with a club and spears,
a temp sent out to do a routine job,
faced toward the whale, and was about to lob.
They'd cheated here and there, bypassing stars.

I could do it better: first I'd just fill
the stars in; the tenuous lines drawn to
and fro between formed the constellations.
How could I help it that the lines I drew
should join to shape a sword, a knee, a tail?
There were no stars skipped, no aberrations.

(translated by Jacob Lowland)

ANNEMARIE FISCHER: PORTRAIT OF ROBBERT

There's a dead pig hanging above his place.
If it's not there, at least it has dripped down
on him. Does he know? Are his eyes open?
His spectacles deprive me of his face.
The glass reflects white, that vouchsafes nothing,
but in the wink of an eye it can be
running over with blood, a white that we
hope will not blind and deafen everything.

He sits behind a table. On it: meat.
It's pork. And more than that: an appendage.
A trotter. With which a human of flesh

and blood sits at the table unafraid.
Something's in between him and me. I read:
an empty table, impeccably white.

(translated by Jacob Lowland)

Annemarie Fischer is a contemporary Dutch painter; *Portrait of Robert* is one of her
better-known paintings.—Translator's Note.

Ad Zuiderent
(1944–   )

RETURN TO SOLITUDE

I went back there this morning and alone.
I hunted words for it: the Houtmankade,
the silence round the piles of new-trimmed lumber
and rows of boats to ply canals and streams.

I knew all this, what was I doing here?
The road came to a stop, no ferry Sundays.
Edge-of-town odors, wind to stay in always,
as if the future were already past.

My dream stands firm, the way the warehouse
stands alongside the water, great with years.
A word turns image, a bikeride turns emotion.
This way leads nowhere. So I cycled back.

(translated by James S Holmes)

Houtmankade: a quay in Amsterdam, named after the sixteenth-century Dutch explorer Cornelis Houtman (his family name means "Woodman"). It leads to the city's timber port, from which there is a ferry across the harbor to Amsterdam North. —Translator's Note.

HOUSE ON THE RIVER

After the rain the bright wide air
burst through high transoms into the room.
You flee down to the basement, set
both the doors open for the heady scent
of rain-wet grass hemmed in by garden walls.

Then everything turns otherwise: you come
out of the sea, your breast heavy with cold,
and stand there on the margin of the shore,
see for the nonce no danger through the wall
of beachgrass beyond which something moves.

Here too, what you see proves not to be true:
the wall fades and your glasses on the desk
reflect the light that slants in from the gardens.
Closing your eyes yields no solution:
the darkness turns to light, the image to pain.

(translated by James S Holmes)

APPEALING TO THE IMAGINATION

I've spent the night at the table
somewhat overwrought, caught, thought, no taut rhyme
supplied me with sufficient softness. The glass
no longer let itself be filled, for I, as if frozen
sat unasleep in weak lamplight.

If noises of cars dissolved in the darkness,
if doors shut tight, then I thought I heard the hall light.
But deaf to the world around me

I saw the door not opening. Forms of you
lay frigid in my head: I sat at the table sans.

Until morning thawed into slow gray
behind the window, passage
without pause. If I haven't thought it
I at least wrought it. Maybe it meant nothing
and you were not standing shaking my shoulder.

(translated by Scott Rollins)

GESTURE OF UNDERSTANDING

Shelter me from the myth, but gesture of
love, hair and hand together solacing.

My understanding's turned to stone; I dreamed
of childhood images. Bring them to life.

It is an ancient tale (from what strange land?)
that if a baby tries to walk too soon

they cut its legs off slantwise above the knee:
truncated torso out of which grows new life,

one with the carpeting in tiny rooms,
united with the lawns in close-walled gardens.

That's to keep peace inside the family,
so you don't have to slap it into shape.

Is your child-rearing dream as strict as that?
Then look me up; I don't quite follow it.

The floor was marble and the torso stone
(years of understanding stood in between).

Touch me then, compassionate of objects,
gesture of myth, carve in the stone my name.

(translated by James S Holmes)

Hans Tentije
(1944–   )

ICARIAN IS THE SEA

Birds gathered for the great black migration
eastwind grabbed me from behind, hoarse swarms flew over
rising water and at my feet, seaweed washed and Icarus
    washed up
deserted stretch of beach between IJmuiden and Wijk aan Zee

o, covered with fuel oil, broken-winged much longer than
    we here
October 13, I could have easily written it down in the sand
with one of his flight feathers if I'd wanted, plus the insane
    year 1973

but even before the wreckmaster came with his swaying cart
on those ungodly pneumatic tires you know, cynically chaw-
    ing tobacco,
a wave had already swept him back, for good and for good

later in The Swan Inn numbed to the bone I tried
dialing Ovid, still exiled, but something kept hounding my
    footsteps
scraping along in my chainguard: story, story without end
headwind and with all that booze I could hardly get the
    pedals to go round

what was I, what was I for god's sake supposed to do with
    the truth?

(translated by Scott Rollins)

IJmuiden, on the North Sea to the west of Amsterdam, is that city's seaport, con-
nected by a ship canal. Wijk aan Zee is a seashore village two miles north of IJmui-
den.—Editors' Note.

BARGES, RIVERS

I
No mountains moved in the heart of the seas
no naiads but autumn, visibility worse

launched, almost falling landed
on the water, barge that is yet to rust from prow
to propeller—its wake dead water in which
what remains vanishes as foam

lying low with sand and with gravel we move
upstream, water spills over the gangway to
the rolled-down tops of my boots

2
Drench me with all that goes by—

"Flemish Spoken Here" it says in
unlearnt italics on the shopfront
near the sluice, here on the Oise, practically Paris

but the Antwerp paper in the window
from a kite-string is days of sailing old

thus falter the moments between arrival
and departure, as between standstill and decay
when the gangplank sags to wretched moss
it's eternally overrun with on the dock

3
What sinks in from looking submerges in water
brackish as sleep, in stilled undercurrents of
time, along banks without horizons

to undergo the total view from such a height
of vineyards and floodlands, the valley below
and not needing to know where it runs aground
in which bend, on which jetties

names like Vistula, Danube, Rhine blow away
flaking off in the light of their own prospect
in vain too the haze of this panorama

4
At times translucent the image right to the grain
like an illusion seen through forever

by chance my freight not subject to spoilage
the shipment confiscated after clearance
the spot you find back, never what happened

only trees, lonely as ever on the opposite bank

without cease without any other prospect
a mirroring that reveals nothing but what there is
to see: the darkness at night and by day
how they lie there once they've been felled

5
No ways bear oblivion so tangibly

on board a returning barge slowly
moving along with the current, it accelerates the end
only in one's mind, and what's the use of the opposite?
smoke mingles unsolvably with dusk

and when my keeshond has pissed near the bilge hole
I hoist him up, rub my fingers through his tangles—
the river remains, as in my sleeping a dream

(translated by Scott Rollins)

Hans Vlek
(1947–   )

FAMINE WINTER

The deed that takes place in winter
is called a poem. The leaky saucepan
on the stove with a leftover of words

to be served hot. How many of them
don't have chapped lips or
blue-stiffened hands or both?
(The wind broken-winged has settled,
sharp though as a razor
blade. The light has
bled dry.)

In the tearoom sits the poet and
stirs the lukewarm pot of emotions round
and round. Sips, blows out the fire
then and heaves a sigh of enlightenment
with a breath like a cloud of ice.

(translated by James S Holmes)

"Famine winter" is a term generally used in the Netherlands to refer to the winter of
1944–45, when the Germans cut off all food transport to the urban west of the coun-
try, with the result that thousands of people died of hunger and many more were on
the point of starvation.—Translator's Note.

NOT FOR SALE

In this small sideroom a lovely
painting in which, squeezed in
inside a row of houses,
a vegetable shop with crates
of fruit on display in the street.

Fruit that even Cézanne
could learn from, cans
of peaches and endives that
put Jasper Johns to shame.

The painting, beneath a strip
of almost white lace curtain, there's
where I buy my groceries, afternoons.
In the frame, at the bottom,
a begonia and two glasses.

(translated by James S Holmes)

DURABLE MATERIAL

I'd like to wrestle free
of matter; the smell of the catbox,
the way that cats-and-dogs weather
affects my humor, the fretting
of the baby for her bottle.

I'd really like to write something
edible even after decades, like
the can of spinach in Scott's tent, something
that doesn't rot straightaway: words,
like death, god, breathing, love—

But death I don't know, god's not
in my circle of friends, and my breathing
is faster when I make love, a thing
I won't describe but would rather
experience with you.

I'd like to move on up
to a higher level, the clouds for instance or
the attic, where the laundry hangs, and the smell
of life forgotten, the smell of matter, and where
a cheery sun through the skylight or a sad rain on the tiles
sweeps the creaking floor with my high intentions.

(translated by James S Holmes)

Jotie T'Hooft
(1956–1977)

LENNY BRUCE FIXES:

Again: who really knows
how smoothly the penis needle glides
into the vagina of the veins
that he shoots full of stiffly
priced seed-cells that inflame
nervous system and cerebral membrane
with a febrile flash
that pales all else
(desires, singularized)
joy, that rings in the ears
and fear that chooses the path
that hares go down whose breathless dash
is finally cut short by a Hunter.

(translated by Scott Rollins)

Likewise in the name of Brian Wilson, Alex Trocchi, Keith Richard, Jimi Hendrix,
Jotie Deadhead, et al.—Author's Note.

STARSHIPS

Starships, yeah sure, metal seed of mankind
Convulsing sent off in a space
In which were forgotten: the galactites
And the Richter scale of the conscience
That has been conscious but wearily forgot.

And that spacesuit (are you all crazy?) fits loosely:
Vacuum-packed peanuts, cans of corned beef
With tender brains, suits of armor full of humbug
Only after mice and monkeys as always: we
Ever cheerful Guru Guru Groove

Fire for the hell of it, go ahead and touch fire
And water and chlorine gas on Jupiter,
It profits you nothing, those bathtubs rot
Into comic dust and precede in this
The earth, interstellar empires,
Human bones.

(translated by Scott Rollins)

LOVE AND MISERY

I've soaked weeks-old bread in water
and eaten it, while the cold
chewed my toes. I've stirred and sought
in my blood with needles. And found nothing.
I've slept on the stones of the street
with a hunger that nothing could still
so it seemed.

In nights wet and dark I was alone
and none heard my voice. Sicknesses
visited me in the years, I wanted to
flee into death.

But nothing was worse than now, I wish
you would come to me and look in my eyes.

(translated by James S Holmes)

POETIC INSTITUTION

The walls are white and the psychiatrists
suspiciously friendly. There's hope
of a cure, but I've never yet
seen anyone leave that didn't come back.

Days that I lose my way on the way to
my own room alternate with days
when I see through the world like a crystal.

Sometimes I wake up shouting.
Sometimes I'm carried off and given
a hypo, sometimes tied down.

There are moments when in a muse I'm
utterly happy for ages:
when I lay my hands on the earth then
they're very small hands.

(translated by James S Holmes)

KICKING THE HABIT

Mucus that runs from your nose your eyes
your mouth and your ears are infected.
Asthmatic spells of coughing that almost
make you heave.
Then vomiting, diarrhea, hot and cold
fever. Headache.

Falling in a deep sleep, waking up
and more misery.
Crawling over the floor, scratching nails
across the walls, groaning.

After three days the worst is over;
you sit at breakfast pale but clean
and already you crave it again.

(translated by James S Holmes)

Notes on the Poets

GERRIT ACHTERBERG (Dutch, 1905–1962) is generally considered to have been the greatest Dutch poet of recent times. A master formal craftsman, he published two dozen books of verse, most of them concerned with a frenetic search for the esoteric juxtaposing of words that would call his dead beloved back to life. In 1949 he was awarded the Dutch State Prize for Literature. A selection from his work in English translation was published as *A Tourist Does Golgotha* (1972).

HANS ANDREUS was the pen name of Johan van der Zant (Dutch, 1926–1977). The most prolific of recent Dutch poets, he published some twenty-eight volumes of verse during his lifetime, as well as a number of other books. His later poetry was much concerned with light as the symbolic life force. In the fifties he also wrote a great many poems in English, a number of which were published in issues of the international review *Botteghe Oscure*.

ARMANDO is the pen name of Herman Dirk van Dodeweerd (Dutch, b. 1929). A painter as well as a poet, he played a central role in the Zero and New Style movements of the late fifties and early sixties. A major concern in his poetry is his attempt to fathom the violence unleashed on Europe by Nazi Germany. In keeping with this, he now lives in Berlin, where he writes a weekly column for a leading Dutch daily.

H. H. TER BALKT (Dutch, b. 1938) grew up on a farm in the east of the Netherlands, and an interest in things agrarian is a central theme in his poetry, which repeatedly contrasts nature and culture in concrete, earthy imagery. After studying Dutch, he now teaches in a secondary school in the university town of Nijmegen. His early poetry was published under the pen name Habakuk II de Balker.

H. C. TEN BERGE (Dutch, b. 1938) began publishing in the mid-sixties, at which time he also founded the prominent Dutch literary review *Raster* (Grid). His interest in ethnopoetics has led him to collect and translate poetry, myths, and fables of the Aztecs, North American Indians, Eskimos, and native Siberians, sources that also provide many of the building blocks for his own complex post-Poundian poetry.

J. BERNLEF is the pen name of Henk Marsman (Dutch, b. 1937). In 1958 he joined K. Schippers to found the magazine *Barbarber* in a reaction against the Experimental group. Fascinated by the art of omission in his nine volumes of poetry, he has a close kinship with the music of Satie and Cage, but also Ives, all three of whom have been subjects of studies he has written. He recently completed a long study of the painter Edward Hopper. American poets he has translated into Dutch include Marianne Moore, William Carlos Williams, and Elizabeth Bishop.

CEES BUDDINGH' (Dutch, b. 1918) began writing poetry before World War II, but it was considered too "light" to be taken seriously until around 1960. He has moved through many forms and styles, usually perversely out of step with the modes of the moment, but his wry humor and very personal tone have remained as constants. He regularly helps to organize the annual Poetry International festival in Rotterdam.

REMCO CAMPERT (Dutch, b. 1929), though one of the Experimental group emerging in the fifties, has always shunned the verbal and stylistic fireworks of his colleagues in favor of an ironic simplicity. He was awarded the Dutch State Prize for Literature in 1976. Two of his novels (*No Holds Barred*, 1965, and *The Gangster Girl*, 1968) and a book of selected poems (*In the Year of the Strike*, 1968) have appeared in English.

HUGO CLAUS (Flemish, b. 1929) is a Jack-of-all-genres, attracted alike to poetry, fiction, and the theater. Three times the winner of the Belgian State Prize for Flemish Literature (twice for a play, once for his poetry), he has been the major literary force in Flanders for a third of a century. His poetry, esoteric and hermetic in the fifties, has sinced become more accessible and engaged. His first novel, *The Duck Hunt*, has appeared in English, and his plays *A Bride in the Morning* and *Friday* have been staged in (respectively) New York and London.

HERMAN DE CONINCK (Flemish, b. 1944) works as a journalist for the Flemish weekly *Humo*. His three books of poems, colloquially sensual in tone, place him in the forefront of the Flemish neo-realist movement which emerged around 1970.

PATRICK CONRAD (Flemish, b. 1945) has made several films and exhibited drawings in Europe and Japan and has written some eighteen books. His highly mannered poetry reflects the elegance of his life as an Antwerp dandy. In 1973 he took the initiative to found the Flemish group of Pink Poets.

JAN G. ELBURG (Dutch, b. 1919) teaches spatial planning at the Rietveld Art Academy in Amsterdam. In the vanguard of Dutch experimentalism even before the emergence of the Experimental group, he writes poetry using a technique that is basically one of montage. His verse, for all its obscurity, is centered on the Marxist principle that art has a social task to perform.

HANS FAVEREY (b. 1933), Surinamese by birth, has lived in the Netherlands since early childhood. He now teaches psychology at the University of Leiden. The poetry of his five volumes to date, turned in on itself, combines words in such a way that established meanings and symbolic values are sheared off. The poems, he posits, at the same time mean everything and nothing.

GUST GILS (Flemish, b. 1924) formed with Pernath and Snoek the Generation of '55, the second experimental generation in Flanders, but he is attracted much more than were the other two to the anecdotal, the grotesque, the slapstick, and the banal. His recent work shows an affinity for various kinds of non-mainstream literature and diverse forms of contemporary music. He has also written songs, plays, and a type of very brief fiction he calls "paraprose."

JACQUES HAMELINK (Dutch, b. 1939) has published twelve volumes of poetry since his debut in the mid-sixties, in them attempting to revivify a mythical consciousness in which the dream is reintegrated with reality. Also well known as a writer of fiction, he has had several books published in French and German translation.

JAN HANLO (Dutch, 1912–1969) was the most Dada-oriented of the Experimental poets. An uncomfortably different member of the fifties group, he found a more congenial niche for his "texts" in the late fifties and the sixties within the review *Barbarber*. His untranslatable nonsense-syllable poem "Oote boe" (Oh taboo!) for years constituted the ordinary person's mistaken notion of Experimental poetry.

FRITZI HARMSEN VAN BEEK (Dutch, b. 1927) was long associated with the poets of the fifties generation before she herself began to publish. The author of two books of verse (and three of prose), she is renowned for her colloquial-cum-baroque syntax and whimsically original themes. She is also an artist, and has illustrated both a book by Komrij and one containing her own fairy tales.

JUDITH HERZBERG (Dutch, b. 1934) is a master of sharp observation and tiny detail. Her seven books of poetry, the first in 1963, have earned her the position of being the foremost woman poet in Dutch. She edited the book *Charlotte,* an autobiography-in-watercolors by the German Jewish painter Charlotte Salomon, and also wrote the scenario for the German-Dutch film *Charlotte* based on Salomon's ill-fated life.

MARK INSINGEL is the pen name of Marcus Donckers (Flemish, b. 1935). After a first volume of "conventional" poetry he moved into the constructivist mode, and is perhaps the finest representative in the Low Countries of the international concrete poetry movement. Four of his novels have appeared in English.

ROLAND JOORIS (Flemish, b. 1936) wrote his early verse under a strong impulse from jazz music, but it is the minimalist preoccupation of his later poetry for which he has become known. Besides his eight volumes of verse he has written several books on contemporary painters.

PIERRE KEMP (Dutch, 1886–1967) published his first book of poetry as long ago as 1914, and before World War II was somewhat known as an eccentric minor poet, eclipsed by a now-forgotten poet brother. Not till the fifties was there any real appreciation for his poetry; this has since come particularly for his playful short verses, hardly ever longer than ten or a dozen lines, of which he wrote thousands, for years at least one a day. He received the Dutch State Prize for Literature in 1959. *An English Alphabet* (1961) is a selection of twenty-six of the short poems in translation, arranged as an abc.

GERRIT KOMRIJ (Dutch, b. 1944) has come to the fore in the seventies as one of the Netherlands' most brilliant poets and translators and sharpest critics and essayists. His verse is characterized by its combination of traditional formal espects (he makes frequent use of the sonnet form) with a contemporary sensibility and an acerbic wit. A selection of his poems has appeared in English translation as *The Comreigh Critter* (1982).

RUTGER KOPLAND is the pen name of the Dutch psychiatrist Rudi van den Hoofdakker (b. 1934), who currently is doing research at the University of Groningen. His eight volumes of poetry are concerned above all with the loss of childhood paradise and the impossible need to reclaim past time. A selection of his poems in English translation has appeared under the title *An Empty Place to Stay* (1977).

GERRIT KOUWENAAR (Dutch, b. 1923) began writing after World War II as a member of the international group of painters and poets called Cobra (Copenhagen-Brussels-Amsterdam). His poetry is obsessed with the nature of words and the slippery relationship between language and reality. Rejecting the poem as a vehicle for the expression of emotion, he seeks to create "the poem as an object." A prolific translator of plays, notably *the* Dutch translator of Brecht, Kouwenaar holds the Martinus Nijhoff Translation Prize (1967) as well as the Dutch State Prize for Literature (1971). He is generally considered the foremost Dutch poet writing today. *Décor/Stills* (1975) is a chapbook containing two of his cycles in English translation.

JAN KUIJPER (Dutch, b. 1947) is an editor for a leading Dutch literary publisher. Considered by many the best of the younger group of poets who write exclusively in the sonnet form, he says of that form that it is "a bow which should be stretched taut with great care and precision." He has published three books of sonnets to date (1973, 1979, 1983).

HANS LODEIZEN (Dutch, 1924–1950) studied biology at Amherst, where he was a friend of James Merrill. He died of leukemia at twenty-six. The first poet in Dutch to exploit the power of the colloquial tone, he was a transitional figure between the prewar poets and those of the fifties, incorporating romantic and surrealistic themes and images in an experimental form that is sometimes reminiscent of e.e. cummings.

LUCEBERT is the pen name of Lubertus J. Swaanswijk (Dutch, b. 1924). The great word-fabricator, spokesman, and crowned Emperor of the generation of the fifties, Lucebert in the later fifties returned to painting as his chief art form, and has since exhibited extensively on both sides of the Atlantic. He was awarded the Dutch State Prize for Literature in 1967. A book of his poetry, texts, and art appeared in 1963 as *Lucebert Edited by Lucebert*, a chapbook of his poems in 1974 as *The Tired Lovers They Are Machines*.

HANNY MICHAELIS (Dutch, b. 1922), after a book of formal, romantic poetry in 1947, in the late fifties developed the form of brief, clear-etched cameos of everyday life which has been the trademark of her poetry since. She worked for many years as secretary to the Amsterdam alderman for the arts and to the Amsterdam Arts Council.

ADRIAAN MORRIËN (Dutch, b. 1912) published his first book of poetry in 1939. Both his verse and his short stories are marked by a luxurious sensuousness unusual among the Dutch. Long the editor of *Literair Paspoort* (Literary Passport), a review of foreign writing, he is now one of an editorial team translating the major works of Freud into Dutch. A selection of his poetry was issued in English translation as *The Use of a Wall Mirror* (1970); several of his short stories have appeared in American reviews.

CEES NOOTEBOOM (Dutch, b. 1933), no doubt the most widely traveled of Dutch poets, is well known in the low countries for his articles and books on faraway places. But he has also written seven books of poetry, six novels, and two plays. In 1982 his novel *Rituals* (English translation 1983) was awarded the international Pegasus Prize. Nooteboom's poetry, however far-ranging its setting, is almost obsessively concerned with the difficulty, the near-impossibility of communication.

HUGUES C. PERNATH was the pen name of Hugo Wouters (Flemish, 1931–1975). For fifteen years a professional soldier, he was a member of the Generation of '55, the second generation of Flemish experimentalists who founded the review *Gard Sivik* (Civic Guard). He was one of the most hermetic of all poets in Dutch, yet through the obscurity one can always hear the cry-from-the-heart of the wounded animal. After his untimely death he was posthumously awarded the Belgian State Prize for Flemish Literature (1977).

SYBREN POLET is the pen name of Sybe Minnema (Dutch, b. 1924). His verse combines the poetic skills developed by the Experimental group with an ongoing fascination with the dubious wonders of present and future technology. He has also written six novels, all highly unorthodox in form. He lived for a time in Stockholm, and has translated extensively from the Swedish. His cycle of poems *X-Man* appeared in English translation in 1979.

PAUL RODENKO (1920–1976), Dutch of Russian parentage, had not read a poem in Dutch until 1947; this unfamiliarity no doubt provided him with such an iconoclastic and original view of the Dutch poetic situation. Better known as an essayist than as a poet, he was the chief critical advocate and apologist for the Experimental movement. In 1977 he was posthumously awarded the leading Dutch prize for critical writing, the Wijnaendts Francken Prize.

BERT SCHIERBEEK (Dutch, b. 1918) as one of the generation of the fifties wrote a series of experimental "novels" that were as much poetry as fiction, but it was not until the seventies that he began publishing self-acknowledged poetry. He has also written travel books and essays on the creative process and on Zen. Schierbeek was Writer in Residence at the University of Michigan in 1981–1982. His book publications in English include *Shapes of the Voice* (1977), an extensive selection from his entire work, and two chapbooks, *The Fall* (1973) and *Mexico I* (1981).

K. SCHIPPERS is the pen name of Gerard Stigter (Dutch, b. 1936). The founder, with Bernlef, of the review *Barbarber,* he was and is fascinated by the ways we experience and classify things. He has written extensively on modern and contemporary art, and has compiled a book-length survey of Dada in the Netherlands. He has also published three experimental novels.

PAUL SNOEK was the pen name of Edmond Schietekat (Flemish, 1933–1981). He was one of the Generation of '55, the second generation of Flemish experimentalists who founded *Gard Sivik* (Civic Guard). There are, he wrote, a baker's dozen key words to his poetry: water, shadow, light, dark, gold, luxury, truth, distance, space, earth, drinking, carrying, becoming. A selection of his poems in English translation was published as the chapbook *In the Sleep-Trap* (1976).

HANS TENTIJE (Dutch, b. 1944) teaches Dutch in a secondary school. In his three books of poetry to date (1975, 1978, 1982) he draws on a varied arsenal of cultural and historical themes in an attempt to congeal "slipping time" and so to preserve unlimited potentialities within the framework of the poem.

JOTIE T'HOOFT (Flemish, 1956–1977) was the first poet in Dutch to write, in excruciatingly straightforward terms, about the pleasures and perils of life as a junkie. A few months after he began working as an editor for a leading Flemish publisher, he died of an overdose of drugs.

HANS VERHAGEN (Dutch, b. 1939) has ranged from the clinically objective in his first volume of poems to a kind of neo-romanticism in more recent verse. Each of his books has been unexpectedly distinct in character; uniting them all is a preference for the poem cycle. A large part of his poetry is available in English translation in the book *Stars over Bombay* (1976). Verhagen works for Dutch television, where he long had his own talk show.

HANS VLEK (Dutch, b. 1947) published his first book of poetry when he was eighteen. His verse in the late sixties was marked by an acute perception of the specific detail; his more recent verse shows an increasing interest in abstraction and things religious.

EDDY VAN VLIET (Flemish, b. 1942) is a lawyer by profession. His poetry, stripped bare of metaphors and complex constructions, is an ongoing examination of the way in which society as it is today impinges on his own individuality in all its vulnerability. The author of six books of poetry, he is also known as a controversial anthologist.

LEO VROMAN (Dutch, b. 1915) is a biologist. After having been a prisoner of war in Indonesia and Japan during World War II he moved to the United States in 1946 and now works at a hospital in Brooklyn. Two major themes in his poetry are his affection for his wife Tineke and the recurrent strangeness of life in the United States. He writes in English as well as Dutch; his *Poems in English* (1953) contained his early verse in his second tongue, and these poems are reprinted, with many later ones, in an English section of his collected *262 Gedichten* (262 Poems, 1974).

HANS WARREN is the pen name of Johannes Menne (Dutch, b. 1921). Both in its tone and its classical and homoerotic themes, his poetry shows a close affinity for that of Kavafis, which he has translated. Living in the southwestern Dutch province of Zeeland, he has served as literary critic for the leading newspaper in the area since 1951. He is an amateur bird watcher and has written a book on night birds.

RIEKUS WASKOWSKY (Dutch, 1932–1977) studied philosophy, and in his three volumes of poetry effected an unusual juxtaposition of philosophical concerns (largely oriented to Kant and Wittgenstein) with such subjects as sex, liquor, and jazz and rock music, all with a strong admixture of idiosyncratic humor.

AD ZUIDERENT (Dutch, b. 1944) teaches Dutch literature at the Free University in Amsterdam, writes criticism for a Dutch weekly, and is an editor of a continuing critical lexicon of contemporary writing in Dutch. In the quiet, low-keyed verse in semiformal patterns of his two latest volumes (his first, published in 1968, was quite different in tone and intent) he attempts to seek out the past in the guise of the ordinary and commonplace. *Cycling, Recycling* (1984) is a book of his poems translated into various languages.

Notes on the Translators and Editors

ANTHONY AKERMAN, born in Durban, South Africa, in 1949, left his native country in 1973. After studying play directing at the Old Vic Theatre School in Bristol, he moved to Amsterdam, where he works as a free-lance director. His first play, *Somewhere on the Border,* was produced in Amsterdam in 1983.

WANDA BOEKE grew up in Massachusetts, where she was born of Dutch parents in 1954. After obtaining an MFA in Translation from the University of Iowa (with a thesis featuring translations of Lodeizen and Ten Berge), in 1979 she went as a Fulbright Scholar to the Netherlands, where she works as a free-lance translator.

JAMES BROCKWAY, born in the United Kingdom in 1916, moved to the Netherlands after serving in World War II. He has published extensively in both the Netherlands and England as a critic; in 1949 his early poetry was collected as *No Summer Song.* Awarded the Martinus Nijhoff Prize for Translation in 1966 for his many translations of Dutch poetry and fiction into English, he has also translated Christopher Isherwood's *A Single Man* into Dutch.

J. M. COETZEE, born in 1940, is a well-known South African novelist who teaches English at the University of Cape Town. His novel *Life and Times of Michael K.* won the coveted Booker Prize in England in 1983. Besides translations of Dutch poetry and fiction he has also published a study of Achterberg's long poem *Ballad of the Gas-Fitter* (in *PMLA,* March 1977).

ADRIAN HENRI, born in 1932, is one of the best-known of the Liverpool group of poets which also includes Brian Patten, Adrian

Mitchell, and Roger McGough. His translation of the poem by Kou-
wenaar was made at a translation workshop during the Rotterdam
Poetry International festival held in 1979.

THEO HERMANS was born in Assent, a small town in Belgium,
in 1948. After studying at Ghent, Essex, and Warwick, then teaching
English at the University of Algiers, he now teaches Dutch at the
University of London. Besides translating a great deal of poetry from
Dutch into English, he has also translated from English and Spanish
into Dutch.

JAMES S HOLMES, born in Iowa in 1924, has lived in Amsterdam
since 1949 and has published a wide range of translations of Dutch
poetry since 1950. In 1956 he became the first foreigner to receive the
Martinus Nijhoff Prize for Translation; from 1958 to 1974 he was
poetry editor of the review *Delta,* which he helped to found. His own
poetry, most of it homoerotic in theme, includes *Nine Hidebound Rimes*
(1978) and *Views of Kent* (1980). He teaches translation studies at the
University of Amsterdam and is widely known as a translation the-
orist.

MARJOLIJN DE JAGER, an American of Dutch parentage, has
published translations from the Dutch, primarily of poems by Hanny
Michaelis, in a number of literary magazines in the United States and
Canada. Several of her translations in *Poet Lore* have received special
awards for excellence.

SHIRLEY KAUFMAN was born in Seattle in 1923. In 1969 she won
the award of the International Poetry Forum for her book of poems
The Floor Keeps Turning. She now lives in Israel and regularly trans-
lates Hebrew literature into English.

GRETA KILBURN, born in 1935, spent much of her life in Aus-
tralia, Canada, and England. She now lives in the Netherlands, where
for the past ten years she has devoted her time to translating Dutch
writing into English. Best known of these translations is her version
of Jan Wolkers' novel *Turkish Delight* (1974).

FRED VAN LEEUWEN, born in Maastricht, in the southeast of the
Netherlands, has worked for more than thirty-five years as a radio

programmer and broadcaster. He also writes extensively as a jour-
nalist. The translations published here are from *An English Alphabet*
(1961), a selection of his versions of poems of Pierre Kemp.

ANDRÉ LEFEVERE was born in Ghent in 1945. After studying at
Ghent and Essex, he now teaches literature at both the University of
Antwerp and the University of Texas. He has published translations
from Greek, French, German, and Dutch into English, as well as a
number of books and articles on translation criticism and theory.

RIA LEIGH-LOOHUIZEN, born in Haarlem, the Netherlands, in
1944, worked as an editor for a Dutch publisher before going to live
with her husband, the American novelist James Leigh, in San Fran-
cisco in 1971. She returned with him in 1980 to the Netherlands, where
she has continued translating Dutch poetry into English. While in San
Francisco, she founded the Twin Peaks Press and brought out books
of poetry by Morriën and Kopland in translation.

JACOB LOWLAND, an American poet who works only in fixed
forms, now lives and writes in Amsterdam. His own poetry includes
The Gay Stud's Guide to Amsterdam and Other Sonnets (1978) and *Billy
Begins* (the first canto of an ottava rima epic in progress titled *Billy
the Crisco Kid*). His translations of Komrij are from the book *The
Comreigh Critter and Other Verse* (1982).

CHARLES McGEEHAN, born in 1934 in New Jersey, is a free-lance
translator who compiled and translated the comprehensive anthology
of Schierbeek's work, *Shapes of the Voice* (1977). His own poetry has
appeared in a number of literary magazines.

ALASDAIR MacKINNON was born in South Wales in 1934 of a
Scottish family. He grew up in the North of England before going
to study English literature and law at Cambridge in the early 1950s.
At present he teaches English at the University of Groningen in the
Netherlands.

GRAHAM MARTIN, born in 1932, has taught French at the Uni-
versity of Edinburgh since 1965. He has published translations from
the French, notably *Anthology of Contemporary French Poetry* (1972),
and, with John Scott, translations from the Chinese and Dutch.

PETER NIJMEIJER, born in Amsterdam in 1947, spent part of his life in London and Ireland, where he translated and actively promoted Dutch poetry. He now again lives in the Netherlands, where he is a well-known poet, translator, and critic. He has published three volumes of his own poetry in Dutch.

RAMÓN E. DU PRÉ, who grew up in the multilingual environment (Dutch, English, Papiamento, and Spanish) of Curaçao, in the Netherlands Antilles, was in the Netherlands for some years in the 1950s, and at that time translated a number of poems from Dutch into English.

JOHANNA H. PRINS was born in Syracuse, New York, of Dutch parents in 1959. After living in the Netherlands for nine years she returned to the United States, where she attended high school and Swarthmore College. She worked on the staff of the *American Poetry Review* before going to Europe, where she first studied at Newnham College, Cambridge, on a Marshall Scholarship, then at the University of Amsterdam as a Fulbright Scholar.

ADRIENNE RICH was born in Baltimore, Maryland, in 1929, and graduated from Radcliffe in 1951. Her poetry has been concerned with social questions, peace in Vietnam, and recently almost wholly with women's rights. In 1974 she was co-winner of the National Book Award for *Diving into the Wreck*. Her most recent book of poems is *A Wild Patience Has Taken Me This Far: Poems 1978–1981*. She lives in Massachusetts, where she edits, with the writer Michelle Cliff, the lesbian-feminist journal *Sinister Wisdom*.

SCOTT ROLLINS was born on Long Island in 1952. He attended Syracuse University, and in 1972 moved to Amsterdam, where he studied at the University of Amsterdam for three years. He edited a literary review called *Dremples* from 1975 to 1979, and founded the small press Bridges Books in 1981. He has translated poetry, prose, and film scripts from Dutch into English. His own poetry has appeared in various little magazines in Europe.

JOHN RUDGE, born in 1945, grew up in Birmingham, England. After graduating from Cambridge he worked as a publisher's representative and spent a year in West Africa. He moved to the Netherlands in 1971 and now works as a free-lance translator of prose and film scripts.

KOOS SCHUUR, who was born in 1915 in Veendam, in the north of the Netherlands, worked for a time as a journalist and was an editor of *Het woord* (The Word), the first literary review to publish work of the Experimentalist Dutch poets. In 1951 he emigrated to Australia, where he remained until 1963. Among his many translations into Dutch are Günter Grass's *The Tin Drum*. His own poetry has been collected as *Gedichten 1940–1960* (Poems 1940–1960), 1961.

JOHN SCOTT is a lecturer in Chinese at the University of Edinburgh and author of the novel *To Kill the Hero* (1966). His translations (with Graham Martin) include *Love and Protest: Chinese Poems* (1972) and Remco Campert's *In the Year of the Strike* (1968). He has also translated two novels by Campert.

WILLIAM JAY SMITH, poet, critic, and translator, is the author of eight books of poetry, two of which were final contenders for the National Book Award. In 1980 he published three books: *The Traveler's Tree: New and Selected Poems; Army Brat: A Memoir;* and *Laughing Time: Nonsense Poems* (a selection of his children's poems). Smith has translated poetry from French, Italian, Spanish, Portuguese, Russian, Swedish, and Hungarian. A former Consultant in Poetry to the Library of Congress (1968–1970), he has received many honors, including in 1972 the Loines Award from the American Academy and Institute of Arts and Letters, which elected him a member in 1975. He lives in New York.

LARRY TEN HARMSEL was born in the Dutch Country of Michigan, and now teaches at Western Michigan University in Kalamazoo. His translations of Lucebert have been published in many American reviews. He is currently writing a novel about Dutch immigrants in Michigan.

PAUL VINCENT, born in Dorking, England, in 1942, studied Dutch at Cambridge University and the University of Amsterdam, and since 1967 has been teaching Dutch at the University of London. He has published a number of books and articles on modern Dutch literature.

JOHN STEVENS WADE (Clysle Stevens) was born in 1927 at Smithfield, Maine. His most recent books of poems are *The Cats in the Colosseum* (1973), *Well Water and Daisies* (1974), and *Each to His Own Ground* (1976). He has published several volumes of translations, including two collections from the Dutch.

CLAIRE NICOLAS WHITE is a novelist, essayist, short-story writer, and poet. Her work has appeared in such magazines as *The Saturday Review, The New Yorker, Atlantic Monthly, Harper's Bazaar, Life,* and *The Paris Review.* She is an editor of *Art World* and is the author of the novel *The Death of the Orange Trees* (1963). She lives on Long Island.

ELIZABETH WILLEMS-TREEMAN was born in Oklahoma. After study at Washington University and Harvard and a stint as editor at Harvard University Press, she lived in Amsterdam for twenty-five years. She has translated a number of art books as well as the work of Simon Carmiggelt, one of the most popular Dutch humorists. She is now again living in Oklahoma, where she is a free-lance translator and editor.

MANFRED WOLF, born in Germany in 1935, fled with his parents to the Netherlands in 1938, then during the Nazi Occupation by way of France and Spain to Curaçao. He studied at Brandeis and Chicago, and since 1956 has been teaching at San Francisco State. He has published three volumes of poetry from the Dutch, as well as a study-with-translations of the early twentieth-century Dutch poet Albert Verwey.

Bibliography and Sources

GENERAL

Listed here are anthologies and special issues of literary reviews devoted to contemporary Dutch writing and issued since World War II. Also included are a few studies of contemporary Dutch poetry.

Adam: International Review (London), vol. 17, no. 196 (July 1949). "Special Number on Dutch Literature," ed. Miron Grindea. Includes 20 poems by 20 poets, mostly prewar.

—— nos. 410/412 (1979). "Literary Grachts: A Second Offering of Dutch Poetry and Prose," ed. Miron Grindea. Includes 13 poems by 12 poets.

Atlantic (Boston), vol. 193, no. 4 (April 1954), pp. 97–170. "Perspective of Holland and Belgium: An *Atlantic* Supplement," ed. Charles J. Rolo. Also published separately. Includes 6 poems by 6 poets, tr. by David Cornel DeJong.

Barnouw, Adriaan, comp. and tr., *Coming After: An Anthology of Poetry from the Low Countries*. New Brunswick, New Jersey: Rutgers University Press, 1948. Covers the entire range of poetry in Dutch, leaving off where *Dutch Interior* begins (Achterberg is the only overlap).

Botteghe Oscure (Rome), no. 15 (Summer 1955), pp. 346–64. "An Anthology of Modern Dutch Poetry," tr. James S Holmes. Also reprinted as *estratto*. 23 poems by 10 prewar and postwar poets.

Carcanet (Oxford), June 1963. "Dutch Poetry Supplement," ed. Rutger Kuin. 27 poems by 9 poets.

Chapman (Hamilton, Lanarkshire, Scotland), vol. 2, nos. 5/6 (1974). "Modern Dutch Writing," guest eds. Paul Brown and Peter Nijmeijer. Includes

30 poems by Paul van Ostayen, Lucebert, Kouwenaar, Claus, Schierbeek, Campert, Elburg, Hamelink, and Verhagen.

Contemporary Literature in Translation (Vancouver), no. 32 (1981). Dutch Issue, ed. Theo Hermans. Includes 43 poems by Kouwenaar, Tentije, Insingel, Claus, Snoek, Ten Berge, Van Vliet, Hamelink, and Bernlef.

Decorte, Bert, et al., eds., *25/50/75: A Bouquet of 50 Dutch Poems in English or French Translation*. Bruges: Orion, 1975; *De Bladen voor de Poëzie*, vol. 1975, no. 6. 50 poems by 50 poets, with Dutch texts plus 26 translations into English, 22 into French, 2 into both.

Delta (Amsterdam), vols. 1–16 (1958–1974). Each issue of this review contains several pages of Dutch-language poetry in English translation.

Delta (Cambridge, England), no. 10 (Autumn 1956), pp. 9–13. "Six Modern Dutch Poems," tr. James S Holmes. By 5 poets.

Dimension (Austin, Texas), Special Issue, 1978. Guest ed. Francis Bulhof. Bilingual survey of current experimental prose and poetry in Dutch, including 18 poems by 9 poets.

Glassgold, Peter, ed., *Living Space: Poems of the Dutch "Fifties."* New York: New Directions, 1979. The largest collection of poems by the Experimental generation: 81 poems by Schierbeek, Elburg, Kouwenaar, Lucebert, Polet, Campert, and Claus.

Greenfield Review (Greenfield Center, New York), vol. 10, nos. 3/4 (Winter/Spring 1983), pp. 6–25. "6 Dutch Poets," sel. Scott Rollins. 20 poems by Andreus, Ter Balkt, Ten Berge, Jooris, Snoek, and Van Vliet.

Helix (Ivanhoe, Australia), nos. 7/8 (1981), pp. 63–90. "Seven Flemish Poets," sel. and intro. Theo Hermans. 29 poems by Claus, Snoek, Jooris, Pernath, Nic van Bruggen, Freddy de Vree, and Van Vliet.

Holmes, James S, *Dutch Poetry*. Hilversum, the Netherlands: Radio Nederland Wereldomroep, 1955. Texts of 13 talks, including 27 poems by 17 twentieth-century poets.

Hopkins, Konrad, and Ronald van Roekel, eds., *Quartet: An Anthology of Dutch and Flemish Poetry*. Paisley, Scotland: Wilfion Books, 1978. 24 poems by Herzberg, Van Vliet, Arie van den Berg, and Patricia Lasoen.

Howard, Dorothy, and Hendrika Ruger, trs., *Under Dutch Skies: A Collection of Poems by Dutch Authors*. Windsor, Ontario: Netherlandic Press, 1981. 12 poems by 11 poets, bilingual.

Indian Pen (Bombay), vol. 28, no. 5 (May 1962), pp. 129–44. "Contemporary Literature in the Netherlands," intro. and sel. H. Klumper. 11 poems by 9 poets.

Kim, De: Literair Pamflet (Amsterdam), no. 5 (1955). Special number: "Dutch Poetry / Niederländische Lyrik," ed. Ludwig Kunz. English selection comprises 9 poems by 9 poets.

Koningsberger, Hans, ed. and tr., *Modern Dutch Poetry*. New York: Netherlands Information Service, n.d. [c. 1956]. 43 poems by 37 poets, mostly prewar. Includes the poems in Koningsberger, ed. & tr., "Nine Modern Dutch Poets," in *New World Writing* (New York), no. 8 (1955), pp. 71–81.

Literary Review (Teaneck, New Jersey), vol. 5, no. 2 (Winter 1961–62). Netherlands Number. Includes 26 poems by 17 poets.

—— vol. 7, no. 3 (Spring 1964). Flanders Number, guest ed. Jan-Albert Goris. Includes 37 poems by 21 poets.

Lovelock, Yann, *The Line Forward: A Survey of Modern Dutch Poetry in Translation*. Amsterdam: Bridges Books, 1984. The first book-length survey of twentieth-century Dutch and Flemish poetry in English. Includes translations of 55 poems.

Modern Poetry in Translation (London), nos. 27/28 (Summer 1976). "Dutch Double Issue," guest eds. James S Holmes and Peter Nijmeijer. 163 poems by 34 poets, mostly postwar, the largest collection to appear in English before *Dutch Interior*.

Netherlands P.E.N. Centre, *Lyrical Holland / La Hollande lyrique / Lyrisches Holland*. Amsterdam & Groningen: Arbeiderspers and five other Dutch publishers, 1954. Translations into English, French, and German; in the English section 16 poems by 14 poets, most of them prewar.

Nijmeijer, Peter, ed., *Four Dutch Poets: Lucebert, Gerrit Kouwenaar, Sybren Polet, Bert Schierbeek*. N.p. [London]: Transgravity Press, 1976. 31 poems.

—— *Four Flemish Poets: Hugo Claus, Paul Snoek, Gust Gils, Hugues C. Pernath*. N.p. [London]: Transgravity Press, 1976. 36 poems.

Poet (Madras, India), vol. 11, no. 9 (September 1970). Dutch Number, guest ed. Peter Nijmeijer. 53 poems by 37 poets.

Poetry (Liverpool), vol. 3, no. 12 (Winter 1952), pp. 2–8. "Some Contemporary Dutch Poets," intro. and tr. James Brockway. 5 poems by 5 poets.

Poetry Australia (Five Dock, N.S.W., Australia), no. 52 (1974). "Post-War Dutch and Flemish Poetry," sel. and intro. R. P. Meijer. 49 poems by 36 poets, bilingual.

Prins, E., and C. M. MacInnes, eds. and trs., *War Poetry from Occupied Holland*. London: privately printed, 1945. 28 poems by 17 identified and 5 anonymous poets.

Prospice (Breakish, Isle of Skye, Scotland), no. 5 (1976), pp. 3–35. "Low Countries Poetry," ed. Theo Hermans. 34 poems by Lucebert, Kouwenaar, Claus, and Ten Berge.

Quarterly Review of Literature (Annandale-on-Hudson, New York), vol. 7, no. 4 (1954), pp. 261–77. "Eight Dutch Poets," comp. Simon Vinkenoog. 14 poems by 8 Experimental poets, the first publication of poems by the group in English.

Roggeman, Willem M., ed., *Ten Modern Poets from Flanders*. Dilbeek, Belgium: Flemish P.E.N. Centre, n.d. [1976]. 30 poems.

Rollins, Scott, ed., *Ten Lowlands Poets*. Amsterdam: Dremples, 1979; *Dremples*, nos. 7/8. 76 poems by Schippers, Kees Ouwens, De Coninck, Zuiderent, Freddy de Vree, Ter Balkt, Arie Gelderblom, Leonard Nolens, and T'Hooft.

Rollins, Scott, and Lawrence Ferlinghetti, eds., *Nine Dutch Poets*. San Francisco: City Lights Books, 1982; Pocket Poets Series, no. 42. 59 poems by Karel Appel, Bernlef, Campert, Jules Deelder, Herzberg, Lucebert, Hans Plomp, Schierbeek, and Simon Vinkenoog.

Schierbeek, Bert, *The Experimentalists*. Amsterdam: Meulenhoff, n.d. [1963]; Art in the Netherlands Series. Study of the group, with main emphasis on the visual artists in it.

Shantih (Brooklyn, New York), vol. 2, no. 4 (Spring/Summer 1973). Special "Modern Dutch Literature" Number, guest ed. E. M. Beekman. Includes 31 poems by Paul van Ostayen, Lucebert, Kouwenaar, Claus, Snoek, Verhagen, Ten Berge, Paul de Vree, Pernath, and Schierbeek.

Snapper, Johan P., *Post-War Dutch Literature: A Harp Full of Nails.* Amsterdam: Delta, 1971. A study in four essays reprinted from the review *Delta;* one essay is "The Word Becoming Flesh: Post-War Dutch Poetry" (pp. 9–22).

Snoek, Paul, and Willem M. Roggeman, sel., *1945–1970: A Quarter Century of Poetry from Belgium* [Flemish volume]. Brussels & The Hague: Manteau, 1970. 50 poems by 49 poets, bilingual, in translations by James S Holmes.

Stuiveling, Garmt, *A Sampling of Dutch Literature: Thirteen Excursions into the Works of Dutch Authors.* Tr. and adapted by James Brockway. Hilversum, the Netherlands: Radio Nederland Wereldomroep, n.d. [c. 1962]. Includes 28 poems by 24 twentieth-century poets.

Translation: The Journal of Literary Translation (New York), vol. 10 (Spring 1983), pp. 179–204. "Post-war Dutch Poetry." 17 poems by 16 poets.

Trends: The P.C.T. Literary Magazine (Paisley, Scotland), vol. 2, no. 4 (1979), pp. 76–111. "Dutch/Flemish Poetry," section ed. Theo Hermans. 26 poems by Snoek, Bernlef, Hamelink, Nic van Bruggen, and Arie Gelderblom.

van Vliet, Eddy, and Willem M. Roggeman, eds., *Poetry in Flanders Now.* Antwerp: Flemish PEN Centre, 1982. 76 poems by 21 poets.

van de Waarsenburg, Hans, comp., *Five Contemporary Dutch Poets.* Merrick, New York: Cross-Cultural Communications, 1979; *Cross-Cultural Review,* no. 2. 13 poems by Bernlef, Ter Balkt, Hans van de Waarsenburg, Frank Koenengracht, and Sjoerd Kuyper, bilingual.

—— *Five Contemporary Flemish Poets.* Merrick, New York: Cross-Cultural Communications, 1979; *Cross-Cultural Review,* no. 3. 15 poems by Snoek, Van Vliet, Conrad, De Coninck, and Patricia Lasoen, bilingual.

Wade, John Stevens, ed. and tr., *Poems from the Lowlands.* Auburn, Maine: The Small Pond, 1966; *The Small Pond,* no. 8. 25 poems by 15 poets.

—— *Waterland: A Gathering from Holland.* Whitehorn, California: Holmgangers Press, 1977. 27 poems by 20 poets.

Wolf, Manfred, ed. and tr., *Change of Scene: Contemporary Dutch and Flemish Poems in English Translation.* San Francisco: Twowindows Press, 1969. 28 poems by 13 poets.

—— *The Shape of Houses: Women's Voices from Holland and Flanders.* Berkeley, California: Twowindows Press, 1974. 29 poems by Herzberg, Michaelis, Harmsen ten Beek, Ellen Warmond, and Patricia Lasoen.

Wolf, Manfred, tr., *Ten Flemish Poems.* San Francisco: Twowindows Press, 1972. By Karel Jonckheere, Ben Cami, Gils, Claus, and Snoek.

Writing in Holland and Flanders (Amsterdam), no. 32 (Summer 1973). Special Number "Directions and Figures in the Poetry of Holland and Flanders," intro. R. L. K. Fokkema. 4 poems each by Lucebert, Kouwenaar, Snoek, Pernath, Vroman, and Kopland.

—— no. 38 (Spring 1981). 53 poems by Herzberg, Ten Berge, Verhagen, Hamelink, Conrad, Van Vliet, Jooris, De Coninck, Faverey, Ter Balkt, and Tentije.

WORKS BY INDIVIDUAL POETS

For each poet included in this anthology there are listed here: (1) the poet's collections of poetry in book form, (2) his or her other major books, and (3) translations into English which have been issued in book form or (in the case of poetry only) have been featured at some length in a periodical or an anthology. Titles of collections of poetry which were later reissued in full in collective volumes have been omitted for the sake of brevity. Publishers for whom no place of publication is listed are or were located in Amsterdam.

The Dutch titles of all poems included in this anthology (except for a few which were written in English) are given in brackets after the titles of the books from which they were drawn; this information forms an extension of the information provided in the Acknowledgments (see pp. xxi–xxvii).

GERRIT ACHTERBERG (1905–1962)

Poetry:
Voorbij de laatste stad (Past the Last Town). The Hague: Daamen / Antwerp: De Sikkel, 1955. Selected poems.
Verzamelde gedichten (Collected Poems). Querido, 1963. [All poems]
Het weerlicht op de kimmen (Lightning on the Horizons). The Hague: Bert Bakker / Querido, 1965. Selected poems.
Blauwzuur (Prussic Acid). The Hague: Bert Bakker, 1969.
Achtergebleven gedichten (Poems Left Behind). Querido, 1980.

Translations:
A Tourist Does Golgotha and Other Poems. Selected and translated by Stan Wiersma. Grand Rapids, Michigan: Being Publications, 1972.
In *Delta* (Amsterdam), Summer 1958, pp. 26–31; *Odyssey Review* (New York / Richmond, Virginia), December 1961, pp. 226–39; *PMLA* (New York), March 1977, pp. 285–96.

HANS ANDREUS (1926–1977)

Poetry:
Verzamelde gedichten (Collected Poems). Bert Bakker, 1983. [All poems]

Other Works:
Bezoek (Visit). Holland, 1960. Novella.
Valentijn (Valentine). Holland, 1960. Novel.
Denise. Holland, 1962. Novel.
Many children's books.

Translations:
In *Botteghe Oscure* (Rome), no. 15 (1955), pp. 359–62, no. 18 (1956), pp. 226–34; *Delta* (Amsterdam), Winter 1959–60, pp. 22–27.

ARMANDO (1929–   )

Poetry:
Verzamelde gedichten (Collected Poems). Rotterdam: Nijgh & Van Ditmar, 1964. [All poems]
Hemel en aarde (Heaven and Earth). Bezige Bij, 1971.
Vorstin der machtelozen (Princess of the Powerless). Bezige Bij, 1972.
De denkende, denkende doden (The Thinking, Thinking Dead). Bezige Bij, 1973.
Het gevecht (The Struggle). Bezige Bij, 1976.
Tucht: Gedichten 1971–1980 (Discipline: Poems 1971–1980). Bezige Bij, 1980.

Other Works:
Dagboek van een dader (Diary of a Culprit). Bezige Bij, 1973. Diary.
Aantekeningen over de vijand (Notes about the Enemy). Bezige Bij, 1981. Essays.
Machthebbers: Verslagen uit Berlijn en Toscane (People in Power: Reports from Berlin and Tuscany). Bezige Bij, 1983. Reportage.

H. H. TER BALKT (1938–   )

Poetry:
Boerengedichten (Rural Poems). Bezige Bij, 1969. ["De kruistocht der dieren"]
Uier van 't Oosten (Udder of the East). Bezige Bij, 1970.
De gloeilampen / De varkens (The Lightbulbs / The Pigs). Harmonie, 1972.
["Elegie van de varkens"]
Groenboek (Green Book). Harmonie, 1973.
Ikonen (Icons). Bezige Bij, 1974. ["De molen"]
Oud gereedschap mensheid moe (Old Tools Weary of Humankind). Harmonie,
1975.
Waar de burchten stonden en de snoek zwom (Where the Castles Stood and the
Pike Swam). Harmonie, 1979.
Machines! Maai ons niet, maai de rogge (Machines! Don't Mow Us, Mow the
Rye). Harmonie, 1982. Selected poems 1969–1979.
Hemellichamen (Heavenly Bodies), Harmonie, 1983. ["Gevonden voorwerpen"]

Translations:
In *Dremples* (Amsterdam), 7/8 (1979), pp. 65–75; *Cross-Cultural Review*
(Merrick, N.Y.), 2 (1979), pp. 15–21.

H. C. TEN BERGE (1938–   )

Poetry:
Gedichten (Poems). Athenaeum, 1969. ["Lied in het landschap gevonden,"
"Groenlands fossiel / een ijzige dichter," "Goldrush"]
De witte sjamaan (The White Shaman). Bezige Bij, 1973.
Va-Banque. Bezige Bij, 1977.
Nieuwe gedichten (New Poems). Bezige Bij, 1981. ["De Hartlaubmeeuw"]
Texaanse elegieën (Texan Elegies). Bezige Bij, 1983.

Other Works:
Poëzie van de Azteken (Poetry of the Aztecs). Bezige Bij, 1972. Anthology.
De dood is de jager: Indiaanse mythen van Noordwest-Amerika (Death Is the Hunter:
Indian Myths from the American Northwest). Bezige Bij, 1974. Anthology.
De raaf in de walvis: Mythen en fabels van de Eskimo (The Raven in the Whale:
Myths and Fables of the Eskimo). Bezige Bij, 1976.
Het meisje met de korte vlechten (The Girl with the Short Braids). Bezige Bij,
1977. Stories.
De beren van Churchill (Churchill's Bears). Bezige Bij, 1978. Novellas.

Siberiese vertellingen (Siberian Tales). Bezige Bij, 1979. Anthology.
Levenstekens & doodssinjalen (Signs of Life & Signals of Death). Bezige Bij, 1980. Essays.
Matglas (Frosted Glass). Athenaeum, 1982. Novel.

Translations:
In *New Directions* (New York), 37 (1978), pp. 134–38; *Chicago Review* (Chicago), Autumn 1979, pp. 20–32; *Contemporary Literature in Translation* (Vancouver), 32 (1981), pp. 34–40.

J. BERNLEF (1937–)

Poetry:
Hoe wit kijkt een Eskimo (How White an Eskimo Looks). Querido, 1970.
Grensgeval (Borderline Case). Querido, 1972.
Brits (Bunk). Querido, 1975.
Zwijgende man (Silent Man). Querido, 1976.
De man in het midden (The Man in the Middle). Querido, 1976.
Gedichten 1960–1970 (Poems 1960–1970). Querido, 1977. ["Het geluid van stof," "Erik Satie," "Oom Karel: Een familiefilmpje"]
Stilleven (Still Life). Querido, 1978. ["De kunst om tweedst te zijn"]
De kunst van het verliezen (The Art of Losing). Querido, 1980.
Alles teruggevonden / Niets bewaard (Everything Found Again / Nothing Saved). Querido, 1982.
Winterwegen (Winter Ways). Querido, 1983. ["Geluk"]

Other Works:
Sneeuw (Snow). Querido, 1973. Fiction.
Meeuwen (Gulls). Querido, 1975. Fiction.
Onder ijsbergen (Among Icebergs). Querido, 1981. Novel.

Translations:
In *Trends* (Paisley, Scotland), vol. 2, no. 4 (1979), pp. 87–94; *Cross-Cultural Review* (Merrick, N. Y.), 2 (1979), pp. 7–14; Scott Rollins and Lawrence Ferlinghetti (eds.), *Nine Dutch Poets* (San Francisco: City Lights, 1982), pp. 21–30.

CEES BUDDINGH' (1918–)

Poetry:
Gedichten 1938–1970 (Poems 1938–1970). Bezige Bij, 1971. [All poems except "Ode aan de Yorkshire Dales" and "Soms, 's avonds"]

Tussen neus en lippen (In Passing). Bezige Bij, 1974.
De wind houdt het droog (The Wind Keeps It Dry). Bezige Bij, 1974.
Het houdt op met zachtjes regenen (It's Stopping Drizzling). Bezige Bij, 1976.
    ["Ode aan de Yorkshire Dales"]
De eerste zestig (The First Sixty). Bezige Bij, 1978. ["Soms, 's avonds"]
De tweede zestig (The Second Sixty). Bezige Bij, 1979.
Verzen van een Dordtse Chinees (Verse of a Dordrecht Chinese). Bezige Bij,
    1980.

Other Works:
Eenvouds verlichte waters: Een inleiding tot de poëzie van Lucebert (Simplicities
    Luminous Waters: An Introduction to the Poetry of Lucebert). Zaandijk,
    the Netherlands: Heijnis, 1960. Essay.
Dagboeknotities (Diary Notes). Bezige Bij. Four volumes to date: 1970, 1972,
    1975, 1978.
Daar ga je, Deibel! en andere verhalen (There You Go, Deibel! and Other Sto-
    ries). Bezige Bij, 1975.

REMCO CAMPERT (1929–   )

Poetry:
Alle bundels gedichten (All the Books of Poetry). Bezige Bij, 1976. Collected
    poetry to 1976. [All poems except "1975" and "Pluksgewijs"]
Theater. Bezige Bij, 1979. ["1975"]
Scenes in Hotel Morandi. Bezige Bij, 1983. ["Pluksgewijs"]

Other Works:
Het leven is vurrukkuluk (Life Is Delicious). Bezige Bij, 1961. Novel.
Liefdes schijnbewegingen (Love's Feints). Bezige Bij, 1963. Novel.
Het gangstermeisje (The Gangster Girl). Bezige Bij, 1965. Novel.
Verzamelde verhalen (Collected Stories). Bezige Bij, 1971.
Na de troonrede (After the Queen's Speech to Parliament). Bezige Bij, 1980.
    Stories.

Translations:
In the Year of the Strike: Selected Poems. Translated by John Scott and Graham
    Martin. Poetry Europe Series, no. 8. London: Rapp & Whiting, 1968. Se-
    lected poems.
In *London Magazine* (London), March 1961, pp. 38–42; *Delta* (Amsterdam),
    Spring 1963, pp. 41–46; Peter Glassgold (ed.), *Living Space: Poems of the
    Dutch "Fiftiers"* (New York: New Directions, 1979), pp. 61–72; Scott Rollins
    and Lawrence Ferlinghetti (eds.), *Nine Dutch Poets* (San Francisco: City
    Lights, 1982), pp. 31–40.

No Holds Barred (Liefdes schijnbewegingen). London: Hart-Davis, 1965. Novel.
The Gangster Girl. London: Hart-Davis, 1968. Novel.

HUGO CLAUS (1929–   )

Poetry:
Gedichten 1948–1963 (Poems 1948–1963). Bezige Bij, 1965. ["Achter tra-
  lies," "Familie," "Marsua," "De moeder," "De man van Tollund"]
Dorothea van Male, *Schola Nostra*. Bezige Bij, 1971. Pseudonymous volume.
Gedichten 1969–1978 (Poems 1969–1978). Bezige Bij, 1979. ["Een kalkoen,"
  "Een duif," "In Flanders Fields," "Isis en de beesten: 1," "Ambush"]
Dertig manieren om een fragment van Alechinsky te zien (Thirty Ways to See an
  Alechinsky Detail). Antwerp: Ziggurat, 1980.
Claustrum. Antwerp: PEP, 1980.
Jan de Lichte. Antwerp: Ziggurat, 1981.
Almanak: 366 knittelverzen (Almanac: 366 Rhymes). Bezige Bij, 1982.

Other Works:
De Metsiers (The Metsiers). Brussels: Manteau, 1950. Novel.
De hondsdagen (Dog Days). Bezige Bij, 1952. Novel.
De koele minnaar (The Cool Lover). Bezige Bij, 1956. Novel.
De zwarte keizer (The Black Emperor). Bezige Bij, 1958. Stories.
Het mes (The Knife). Bezige Bij, 1961. Stories.
De verwondering (The Wonderment). Bezige Bij, 1962. Novel.
Omtrent Deedee (Regarding Deedee). Bezige Bij / Antwerp: Ontwikkeling,
  1963. Novel.
Karel Appel, schilder (Karel Appel, Painter). Strengholt, 1964. Essay.
Louis-Paul Boon. Brussels: Manteau, 1964. Essay.
De legende en . . . avonturen van Uilenspiegel . . . (The Legend and Adven-
  tures of Eulenspiegel). Bezige Bij, 1965. Drama.
De dans van de reiger (The Heron's Dance). Bezige Bij, 1966. Film scenario.
Acht toneelstukken (Eight Plays). Bezige Bij, 1966. Drama.
De vijanden (The Enemies). Bezige Bij / Antwerp: Contact, 1967. Film novel.
Morituri. Bezige Bij, 1968. Drama.
Vrijdag (Friday). Bezige Bij, 1969. Drama.
Natuurgetrouwer (More True to Nature). Bezige Bij, 1969. Stories.
Tand om tand (A Tooth for a Tooth). Bezige Bij, 1970. Drama.
Het leven en de werken van Leopold II (The Life and Works of Leopold II).
  Bezige Bij, 1970. Drama.
Schaamte (Shame). Bezige Bij, 1972. Novel.
Het jaar van de kreeft (The Year of the Crab). Bezige Bij, 1972. Novel.
De groene ridder (The Green Knight). Three volumes. Thomas Rap / Bezige
  Bij, 1972, 1973. Stories.

Pas de deux. Bezige Bij, 1973. Drama.
Thuis (At Home). Bezige Bij, 1975. Drama.
De vluchtende Atalanta (Fleeing Atalanta). Antwerp: PEP, 1977. Story.
Het huis van Labakos (The House of Labakos). Bezige Bij, 1977. Drama.
Jessica! Antwerp: Ziggurat / Bezige Bij, 1977. Novel.
Het verlangen (Desire). Bezige Bij, 1978. Novel.
De verzoeking (The Temptation). Antwerp: PEP, 1980 / Bezige Bij, 1981. Story.
Het haar van de hond (The Hair of the Dog). Antwerp: PEP / Bezige Bij, 1982. Drama.
Het verdriet van België (Belgium's Sorrow). Bezige Bij, 1983. Novel.

Translations:
With Karel Appel, *Love Song.* New York: Abrams, 1963.
Selected Poems 1953–1973. Ed. Theo Hermans. Portree, Isle of Skye, Scotland: J.C.R. Greene, 1984.
In *Delta* (Amsterdam), Autumn 1958, pp. 41–46; Peter Nijmeijer (ed.), *Four Flemish Poets* (London: Transgravity Press, 1976), pp. 7–16; Peter Glassgold (ed.), *Living Space: Poems of the Dutch "Fifties"* (New York: New Directions, 1979), pp. 73–84; *Contemporary Literature in Translation* (Vancouver), 32 (1981), pp. 24–27.
The Duck Hunt. New York: Random House, 1955. Paperback editions as *Sisters of Earth.* Novel.
Karel Appel, Painter. New York: Abrams, 1963. Essay.
Friday. London: Davis-Poynter, 1972. Drama.

HERMAN DE CONINCK (1944–   )

Poetry:
De lenige liefde (Lithe Love). Bruges: Desclée de Brouwer / Utrecht: Noorderlicht, 1969. ["Ars poetica: 4," "Frédérique, of hoe ik geschiedschrijver werd," "Zo is hier elke dag"]
Zolang er sneeuw ligt (As Long as There's Snow Lying). Bruges: Orion / Van Oorschot, 1975. ["De rinoceros," "Een Brit"]
Met een klank van hobo (With a Sound like an Oboe). Bruges: Orion / Van Oorschot, 1980. ["Moeder"]

Other Work:
Over troost en pessimisme (On Consolation and Pessimism). Manteau, 1983. Criticism.

Translations:
In *Dremples* (Amsterdam), 7/8 (1979), pp. 33–43.

PATRICK CONRAD (1945–)

Poetry:
Conrad Life on Stage: Gedichten 1963–1973 (Poems 1963–1973). Brussels: Manteau, 1973. [All poems]
Continental Hotel, of De duisternis der dingen loert (Continental Hotel, or The Obscurity of Things Lies in Wait). Antwerp: PEP / Arbeiderspers, 1975.
La mort s'appelle bonsoir (Death Is Named Good Evening). Antwerp: PEP / Arbeiderspers, 1977.

Other Work:
Allegria! Allegria! Brussels: Manteau, 1972. Stories.

Translations:
In *Cross-Cultural Review* (Merrick, N. Y.), 3 (1979), pp. 23–29.

JAN G. ELBURG (1919–)

Poetry:
Gedichten 1950–1975 (Poems 1950–1975). Bezige Bij, 1975. [All poems]
De kikkers van Potter (Potter's Frogs). Bezige Bij, 1981.

Translations:
In *Delta* (Amsterdam), Spring 1964, pp. 23, 26–30, 68; Peter Glassgold (ed.), *Living Space: Poems of the Dutch "Fiftiers"* (New York: New Directions, 1979), pp. 13–24.

HANS FAVEREY (1933–)

Poetry:
Chrysanten, roeiers (Chrysanthemums, Rowers). Bezige Bij, 1977. [All poems]
Gedichten (Poems). Bezige Bij, 1980. Collects *Gedichten* (1968) and *Gedichten 2* (1972).
Lichtval (Lightfall). Bezige Bij, 1981.
Zijden kettingen (Chains of Silk). Bezige Bij, 1983.

GUST GILS (1924–)

Poetry:
Ziehier een dame (Behold a Lady). De Beuk, 1957.
Anoniem 20ste eeuw (Anonymous Twentieth Century). Antwerp: Ontwikkeling, 1959.

Gewapend oog (Armed Eye). Meulenhoff, 1962.
Drie partituren (Three Scores). Bezige Bij, 1962. ["Hoe schoon nietwaar het land des zondags," "Sprookje," "Ballade van een eeuwig misbegrepen man"]
Een plaats onder de maan (A Place under the Moon). Bezige Bij, 1965.
Insomnia Ferox. Sint-Niklaas, Belgium: Paradox Press, 1965.
Manuskript gevonden tijdens achtervolging (Manuscript Found during Pursuit). Bezige Bij, 1967.
Levend voorwerp (Living Object). Bezige Bij, 1969.
Afschuwelijke roze yogurtman (Terrible Pink Yogurt Man). Bezige Bij, 1972.
Linke Kornak (Handy Kornak). Ertvelde, Belgium: Van Hyfte & De Coninck, 1974.
Zevenmaal zeven haikoes (Seven Times Seven Haikus). Antwerp: Soethoudt, 1975.
Little Annie's Lonely Songbook. Antwerp: Soethoudt, 1975.
Een handvol ingewanden (A Handful of Entrails). Bezige Bij, 1977. ["De verslinding van de aarde," "Die goeie goddelijke markies"]
Sneldrogende poëzie (Quick-Drying Poetry). Brussels: Manteau, 1978.
Onzachte Landing (Hard landing). Bezige Bij, 1979.
Uniek onkruid (Unique Weeds). Antwerp: Manteau, 1982.
Een vingerknip (A Snap of the Fingers). Bezige Bij, 1983.

Other Works:
Met de noorderzon op stok (To Roost with the Northern Sun). Zaandijk, the Netherlands: Heijnis, 1960. Stories.
Paraproza (Paraprose). Five volumes. Bezige Bij, 1964, 1966, 1977, 1978, 1980. Stories.
Bericht om bestwil (Notice for Your Own Good). Meulenhoff, 1968. Stories.
Kafka in de onderwereld (Kafka in the Underworld). Antwerp: Ziggurat, 1978. Stories.

Translations:
In Peter Nijmeijer (ed.), *Four Flemish Poets* (London: Transgravity Press, 1976), pp. 27–36.

JACQUES HAMELINK (1939–   )

Poetry:
De eeuwige dag (The Eternal Day). Polak & Van Gennep, 1964.
Een koude onrust (A Cold Uneasiness). Polak & Van Gennep, 1967.
Oudere gronden (Older Grounds). Van Gennep, 1969.
Geest van spraak en tegenspraak (Spirit of Speech and Contradiction). Van Gennep, 1971.
Windwaarts, wortelher (Windwards, Roothither). Van Gennep, 1973.

Witvelden, inscripties (White Fields, Inscriptions). Van Gennep, 1974.
Hersenopgang (Brain Entrance). Van Gennep, 1975.
Niemandsgedichten, 1964–1975 (No Man's Poems). Bezige Bij, 1976. Selected poems.
Stenen voor mijzelf (Stones for Myself). Bezige Bij, 1977. ["Pyreneeën: 1, 6," "Steenspraak"]
Het rif (The Reef). Bezige Bij, 1979. ["Voor de schaduw," "De ammoniet"]
Responsoria. Bezige Bij, 1980.
Ceremoniële en particuliere madrigalen (Ceremonial and Private Madrigals). Bezige Bij, 1982.

Other Works:
Het plantaardig bewind (The Vegetable Reign). Polak & Van Gennep, 1964. Stories.
Horror vacui. Polak & Van Gennep, 1966. Stories.
De rudimentaire mens (The Rudimentary Man). Van Gennep, 1968. Stories.
Ranonkel (Ranuncle). Van Gennep, 1969. Novel.
De betoverde bruidsnacht (The Enchanted Wedding Night). Bezige Bij, 1970. Play.
De boom Goliath (The Tree Goliath). Bezige Bij, 1973. Stories.
Afdalingen in de ingewanden (Descents into the Guts). Bezige Bij, 1974. Stories.
Een reis door het demiurgenrijk (A Trip through the Realm of the Demiurges). Bezige Bij, 1976. Novel.
De droom van de poëzie (The Dream of Poetry). Bezige Bij, 1978. Essay.
Gehandhaafde verhalen (Stories Retained). Bezige Bij, 1979. Stories.
In een lege kamer een garendraadje (In an Empty Room a Silken Thread). Bezige Bij, 1980. Essay.

JAN HANLO (1912–1969)

Poetry:
Verzamelde gedichten (Collected Poems). Van Oorschot, 1958. [All poems]

Other Works:
In een gewoon rijtuig (In an Ordinary Carriage). Van Oorschot, 1966. Miscellanea.
Go to the Mosk. Van Oorschot, 1971. Letters.
Zonder geluk valt niemand van het dak (No One Falls from the Roof unless He's Lucky). Van Oorschot, 1972. Autobiographical novella.
Mijn benul (My Notion). Van Oorschot, 1974. Essays and texts.

FRITZI HARMSEN VAN BEEK (1927–   )

Poetry:
Geachte Muizenpoot (Dear Mousepaw). Bezige Bij, 1965. [Both poems]
Kus of ik schrijf (Kiss or I'll Write). Bezige Bij, 1975.

JUDITH HERZBERG (1934–   )

Poetry:
Zeepost (Sea Mail). Van Oorschot, 1963. ["Katje," "Magie," "Bij een foto"]
Beemdgras (Meadow Grass). Van Oorschot, 1968. ["Begraven," "Beroeps-keuze," "Jiddish," "Afwasmachine"]
Vliegen (Flies). Harmonie, 1970.
Strijklicht (Grazing Light). Van Oorschot, 1971. ["Een kinderspiegel," "Beer in bed," "Gympies"]
27 liefdesliedjes (27 Love Songs). Harmonie, 1971.
Botshol. Van Oorschot, 1980. ["Boomchirurg"]

Other Works:
Dat het 's ochtends ochtend wordt / De deur stond open (That Morning Comes in in the Morning / The Door Was Open). Harmonie, 1974. Two plays.
Het maken van gedichten en het praten daarover (Making Poems and Talking About It). The Hague: Bzztôh, 1977. Essay.
Charlotte: Dagboek bij een film (Charlotte: Diary while Making a Film). Harmonie, 1981.

Translations:
In Manfred Wolf (translator), *The Shape of Houses: Women's Voices from Holland and Flanders* (Berkeley: Twowindows Press, 1974), pp. [5]–[12]; Konrad Hopkins and Ronald van Roekel (eds.), *Quartet* (Paisley, Scotland: Wilfion Books, 1978), pp. 1–14; Scott Rollins and Lawrence Ferlinghetti (eds.), *Nine Dutch Poets* (San Francisco: City Lights, 1982), pp. 53–62.

MARK INSINGEL (1935–   )

Poetry:
Drijfhout (Driftwood). Deurle, Belgium, & Ghent: Colibrant, 1963.
Een kooi van licht (A Cage of Light). Deurle, Belgium, & Ghent: Colibrant, 1966. ["De tuinen, aan nieuwsgierigen verraden"]
Perpetuum Mobile. Meulenhoff, 1969.
Modellen (Models). Meulenhoff, 1970.

Posters. Bruges: Orion / The Hague: Scheltens & Giltay, 1974. ["Met geheven hoofd"]
Het is zo niet zo is het (It's Not So It Is So). Jimmink, 1978.

Other Works:
Een getergde jager (A Tormented Hunter). Meulenhoff, 1966. Stories.
Spiegelingen (Reflections). Meulenhoff, 1968. Novel.
Een tijdsverloop (A Course of Time). Meulenhoff, 1970. Novel.
Dat wil zeggen (That Is to Say). The Hague: Nijgh & Van Ditmar, 1974. Audio-text.
Wanneer een dame een heer de hand drukt . . . (When a Lady Shakes Hands with a Gentleman). Malperthuis, 1975. Prose and audio-texts.
Gezwel van wortels (Swelling of Roots). Jimmink, 1978. Novel.
Mijn territorium (My Territory). Haarlem: In de Knipscheer, 1981. Novel.

Translations:
In *Delta* (Amsterdam), Spring 1973, pp. 91–97.
Reflections. New York: Red Dust, 1972. Novel.
A Course of Time. New York: Red Dust, 1977. Novel.
When a Lady Shakes Hands with a Gentleman & My Territory. New York: Red Dust, 1983. Novels.

ROLAND JOORIS (1936–   )

Poetry:
Gedichten 1958–1978 (Poems 1958–1978). Antwerp: Lotus, 1978. [All poems]
Akker (Field). Tielt, Belgium: Lannoo, 1983.

Other Work:
Atelier: Gesprekken met beeldende kunstenaars (Studio: Conversations with Artists). Ghent: Yang, 1975.

Translations:
In *Helix* (Ivanhoe, Australia), 7/8 (1981), pp. 3–6.

PIERRE KEMP (1886–1967)

Poetry:
Verzameld werk (Collected Works). Three volumes. Van Oorschot, 1976. [All poems]

Translations:
An English Alphabet: Twenty-Six Poems. Translated by Fred van Leeuwen.
   Spectatorpers, 1961.

GERRIT KOMRIJ (1944–   )

Poetry:
Fabeldieren (Fabled Animals). Arbeiderspers, 1975. ["De draken," "De een-
   hoorn," "Het Komrij-wezen"]
Het schip "De Wanhoop" (The Ship *Despair*). Arbeiderspers, 1979. ["Vrucht-
   baar," "De thuiskomst"] ·
Alle vlees is als gras / Ik heb goddank twee goede longen (All Flesh Is as
   Grass / Thank God I've Got Two Good Lungs). Meulenhoff, 1981. ["Op
   je rug," "De vrouw in de kunst," "Een namiddag"]
Gesloten circuit (Closed Circuit). Arbeiderspers, 1982.
De os op de klokketoren (The Bull on the Belltower). Arbeiderspers, 1982.

Other Works:
Verwoest Arcadië (Devastated Arcadia). Arbeiderspers, 1981. Essays.
Het chemisch huwelijk (In Chemick Wedlock). Arbeiderspers, 1983. Verse
   drama.

Tranlations:
The Comreigh Critter and Other Verse. Translated by Jacob Lowland. Amster-
   dam and New York: C. J. Aarts, 1982. Selected poems, bilingual.

RUTGER KOPLAND (1934–   )

Poetry:
Onder het vee (Among the Livestock). Van Oorschot, 1966.
Het orgeltje van yesterday (Yesterday's Organ). Van Oorschot, 1968. ["John-
   son Brothers Ltd"]
Alles op de fiets (Everything by Bike). Van Oorschot, 1972. ["Oud buiten,"
   "Jonge sla"]
Wie wat vindt heeft slecht gezocht (Who Finds Something Has Not Really
   Hunted). Van Oorschot, 1972. ["Tussen de bloemen," "Blackbird," "Geen
   generatie," "Nog eenmaal Tarzan"]
Een lege plek om te blijven (An Empty Place to Stay). Van Oorschot, 1975.
Al die mooie beloften (All Those Nice Promises). Van Oorschot, 1979. ["G,
   ik schreef een vers"]
Dit uitzicht (This View). Van Oorschot, 1982. ["Gesprek"]
[Uncollected: "Dode vogels"]

Translations:
An Empty Place to Stay & Other Selected Poems. Translated by Ria Leigh-Loo-
huizen. San Francisco: Twin Peaks Press, 1977.
In *American Poetry Review* (Philadelphia), January/February 1979, pp. 44–45.

GERRIT KOUWENAAR (1923–)

Poetry:
Gedichten 1948–1977 (Poems 1948–1977). Querido, 1982. [All poems]
Het blindst van de vlek (The Blindest of the Spot). Querido, 1982.

Other Works:
Ik was geen soldaat (I Was No Soldier). Querido, 1950. Novel.
Val, bom (Fall, Bomb). Querido, 1956. Novel.

Translations:
Décor / Stills. Translated by Peter Nijmeijer. Deal, Kent: Actual Size Press,
1975.
In *Delta* (Amsterdam), Spring 1968, pp. 59–62; Peter Nijmeijer (ed.), *Four
Dutch Poets* (London: Transgravity Press, 1976), pp. 21–35; *Dremples*
(Amsterdam), 4 (1976), pp. 20–34; Peter Glassgold (ed.), *Living Space: Poems
of the Dutch "Fiftiers"* (New York: New Directions, 1979), pp. 25–36;
Montemora (New York), 5 (1979), pp. 196–212. *Contemporary Literature in
Translation* (Vancouver), 32 (1981), pp. 11–14.

JAN KUIJPER (1947–)

Poetry:
Sonnetten (Sonnets). Querido, 1973. [All poems]
Oogleden (Eyelids). Querido, 1979.
Bijbelplaatsen (Bible Places). Querido, 1983.

HANS LODEIZEN (1924–1950)

Poetry:
Gedichten (Poems). Van Oorschot, 1952. [All poems]
Nagelaten werk (Posthumous Works). Van Oorschot, 1969.

Translations:
In *Delta* (Amsterdam), Winter 1958–59, pp. 74–79; *London Magazine* (Lon-
don), February 1960, pp. 38–42.

LUCEBERT (1924–   )

Poetry:
Verzamelde gedichten (Collected Poems). Two volumes. Bezige Bij, 1974. [All poems except "Breyten Breytenbach" and "Indigo-eter"]
Oogsten in de dwaaltuin (Harvests in the Labyrinthine Garden). Bezige Bij, 1981. ["Breyten Breytenbach mag de maan zien," "De indigo-eter"]
De moerasruiter uit het paradijs (The Swamp Knight from Paradise). Bezige Bij, 1982.

Translations:
Lucebert Edited by Lucebert. Translated by James S Holmes. London: Marlborough Fine Art, 1963.
The Tired Lovers They Are Machines. Translated by Peter Nijmeijer. New Selection Series. London: Transgravity Press, 1974.
In *Delta* (Amsterdam), Autumn 1968, pp. 81–88; *Dremples* (Amsterdam), 2 (1975), pp. 20–34; Peter Nijmeijer (ed.), *Four Dutch Poets* (London: Transgravity Press, 1976), pp. 7–19; Peter Glassgold (ed.), *Living Space: Poems of the Dutch "Fifties"* (New York: New Directions, 1979), pp. 37–48; Scott Rollins and Lawrence Ferlinghetti (eds.), *Nine Dutch Poets* (San Francisco: City Lights, 1982), pp. 63–76.

Study:
J. Eijkelboom, *Lucebert.* Art and Architecture in the Netherlands Series. Meulenhoff, 1964.

HANNY MICHAELIS (1922–   )

Poetry:
Klein voorspel (Brief Prelude). Van Oorschot, 1949.
Water uit de rots (Water from Stone). Van Oorschot, 1957. ["Eierschalen"]
Tegen de wind in (Into the Wind). Van Oorschot, 1962. ["Onwillekeurig"]
Onvoorzien (Unexpected). Van Oorschot, 1966. ["Wekkerkabaal"]
De rots van Gibraltar (The Rock of Gibraltar). Van Oorschot, 1969. ["Driehoog," "Onachterhaalbaar," "Het lichaam," "Briljant filosoferend"]
Wegdraven naar een nieuw Utopia (Trotting Off to a New Utopia). Van Oorschot, 1971. ["Ergens in huis"]

ADRIAAN MORRIËN (1912–   )

Poetry:
Verzamelde gedichten (Collected Poems). Van Oorschot, 1961.

Moeders en zonen (Mothers and Sons). Van Oorschot, 1962. ["Gastronomie," "Schipbreuk"]
Het gebruik van een wandspiegel (The Use of a Wall Mirror). Van Oorschot, 1968. ["Ouder huis," "Het gebruik van een wandspiegel"]
Avond in een tuin (Evening in a Garden). Van Oorschot, 1980.

Other Works:
Mens en engel (Man and Angel). Bezige Bij, 1964. Stories.
Cryptogram. Van Oorschot, 1968. Notes and essays.

Translations:
The Use of a Wall Mirror. Translated by Ria Leigh-Loohuizen. San Francisco: Twowindows Press, 1970.

CEES NOOTEBOOM (1933–   )

Poetry:
Vuurtijd, ijstijd: Gedichten 1955–1983 (Fire Age, Ice Age: Poems 1955–1983). Arbeiderspers, 1984. [All poems]

Other Works:
Philip en de anderen (Philip and the Others). Querido, 1955. Novel.
De verliefde gevangene (The Enamored Prisoner). Querido, 1958. Novel.
De zwanen van de Theems (The Swans of the Thames). Querido, 1959. Play.
De ridder is gestorven (The Knight Has Fallen). Querido, 1963. Novel.
Een middag in Bruay (An Afternoon in Bruay). Bezige Bij, 1963. Travel.
Een nacht in Tunisië (A Night in Tunisia). Bezige Bij, 1965. Travel.
De Parijse beroerte (The Paris Uprisings). Bezige Bij, 1968. Reportage.
Bitter Bolivia / Maanland Mali (Bitter Bolivia / Moonland Mali). Bezige Bij, 1971. Travel and reportage.
Een avond in Isfahan (An Evening in Isfahan). Arbeiderspers, 1978. Travel.
Rituëlen (Rituals). Arbeiderspers, 1980. Novel.
Voorbije passages (Passages Past). Arbeiderspers, 1981. Travel.
Een lied van schijn en wezen (A Song of Shadow and Substance). Arbeiderspers, 1981. Novel.
Mokusei! Een liefdesverhaal (Mokusei! A Love Story) Arbeiderspers, 1982. Novella.
Gyges en Kandules: Een koningsdrama (Gyges and Kandules: A Royal Drama). Arbeiderspers, 1982. Play.

Translation:
Rituals. Baton Rouge: Louisiana State University Press, 1983.

HUGUES C. PERNATH (1931–1975)

Poetry:
Verzameld werk (Collected Works). Antwerp: PEP, 1980. [All poems]

Other Work:
With Paul Snoek, *Soldatenbrieven* (Soldiers' Letters). Antwerp: Ontwikkeling / Bezige Bij, 1961.

Translations:
Postscript to Today and Other Poems. Translated by James S Holmes. Delta, 1964.
In Peter Nijmeijer (ed.), *Four Flemish Poets* (London: Transgravity Press, 1976), pp. 37–47.

SYBREN POLET (1924–   )

Poetry:
Persoon / Onpersoon (Person / Unperson). Bezige Bij, 1971. ["Aliënatie & alliteratie"]
Illusie & illuminatie (Illusion & Illumination). Bezige Bij, 1975. ["Ideeën van morgen"]
Gedichten I (Poems I). Bezige Bij, 1977. ["Schaduw," "Feestdag," "Heropvoeding," "The Human Use of Human Beings"]
Taalfiguren I & II (Language Figures I & II). Bezige Bij, 1983.

Other Works:
Breekwater (Breakwater). Bezige Bij, 1961. Novel.
Verboden tijd (Forbidden Time). Bezige Bij, 1964. Novel.
Mannekino. Bezige Bij, 1968. Novel.
De sirkelbewoners (The Circle Dwellers). Bezige Bij, 1970.
De geboorte van een geest (The Birth of a Spirit). Bezige Bij, 1974.
Xpertise of De exports en het rode lampje (Xpertise, or The Exports and the Red Light). Bezige Bij, 1978.
De poppen van het Abbekerker wijf (The Abbekerk Woman's Dolls). Bezige Bij, 1983. Prose text.

Translations:
X-Man. Translated by Peter Nijmeijer. London: Transgravity Press, 1979.
In *Delta* (Amsterdam), Autumn 1964, pp. 23–29, 78; *Chelsea Review* (New York), 20/21 (May 1967), pp. 5–10; Peter Nijmeijer (ed.), *Four Dutch Poets* (London: Transgravity Press, 1976), pp. 37–49; Peter Glassgold (ed.), *Living Space: Poems of the Dutch "Fiftiers"* (New York: New Directions, 1979), pp. 49–60.

PAUL RODENKO (1920–1976)

Poetry:
Orensnijder tulpensnijder (Ear Trimmer Tulip Trimmer). Harmonie, 1975.
Collected poems. [All poems]

Other Works:
Over Hans Lodeizen (On Hans Lodeizen). The Hague: Daamen, 1954. Essay.
Tussen de regels: Wandelen en spoorzoeken in de moderne poëzie (Between the
Lines: Walking and Looking for the Trail in Modern Poetry). The Hague:
Daamen / Antwerp: De Sikkel, 1956. Essay.
Op het twijgje der indigestie (On the Twig of Indigestion). Meulenhoff, 1976.
Essays.

Translation:
Fire beside the Sea. Translated by James S Holmes and Hans van Marle.
IJmuiden, the Netherlands: Hoogovens, 1961. Verse cycle.

BERT SCHIERBEEK (1918–   )

Poetry:
De deur (The Door). Bezige Bij, 1972. ["De dood, zei Remco," "Vogel zingt"]
In- en uitgang (The Way In and Out). Bezige Bij, 1975. ["Ishi," "De zon:
dag," "De zon: nacht"]
Weerwerk (Keeping It Up). Bezige Bij, 1977.
Betrekkingen (Relations). Bezige Bij, 1979.
Een tik tegen de lucht (A Tap against the Air). De Populier, 1979.
Binnenwerk (Inside Out). Bezige Bij, 1982,

Other Works:
Een grote dorst (A Great Thirst). Bezige Bij, 1968. Compositional novel. ["Kijk
er komt een man en koopt een paard in Kansas"]
Verzameld werk (Collected Works). Four volumes to date. Bezige Bij, 1978,
1979, 1982, 1983. Primarily compositional novels. ["Leg ik de dag vast"]

Translations:
A Beast-Drawn Man. Translated by John Vandenbergh. Bezige Bij, 1962.
The Fall. Translated by Charles McGeehan. London: Transgravity Press, 1973.
Shapes of the Voice: Epic and Lyric Themes of a (Dutch) Poet. Edited and trans-
lated by Charles McGeehan. Boston: Twayne, 1977.
Mexico I. Translated by Charles McGeehan. Bridges Books, 1981.
In Peter Nijmeijer (ed.), *Four Dutch Poets* (London: Transgravity Press, 1976),
pp. 51–62; Peter Glassgold (ed.), *Living Space: Poems of the Dutch "Fifiers"*
(New York: New Directions, 1979), pp. 1–12; Scott Rollins and Lawrence

Ferlinghetti (eds.), *Nine Dutch Poets* (San Francisco: City Lights, 1982), pp. 89–100.
A Big Dead Beast. Bezige Bij, 1963. Drama.

K. SCHIPPERS (1936–   )

Poetry:
De waarheid als De koe (The Truth as The Cow). Querido, 1963.
Een klok en profil (A Clock in Profile). Querido, 1965. ["Bianca's eerste kunsten"]
Verplaatste tafels: Reportages, research, vaudeville (Shifted Tables: Reportages, Research, Vaudeville). Querido, 1969. ["Puzzels," "Een steen voor Krazy Kat"]
Sonatines door het open raam: Gedichten bij partituren van Clementi, Kuhlau en Lichner (Sonatinas through the Open Window: Poems to Scores by Clementi, Kuhlau, and Lichner). Querido, 1972. ["Zandkorrels op een radio," "Hoe een gitaar op een stoel kan liggen"]
Een vis zwemt uit zijn taalgebied: Tekst en beeld voor witte clown (A Fish Swims out of Its Language Area: Text and Image for White Clown). Querido, 1976.
Een leeuwerik boven een weiland: Een keuze uit de gedichten (A Lark above a Meadow: A Selection from the Poems). Querido, 1980. Selected poems.

Other Works:
Een avond in Amsterdam (An Evening in Amsterdam). Querido, 1971. Novel.
Holland Dada. Querido, 1974. Documentary study.
Bewijsmateriaal (Evidence). Querido, 1978. Novel.
Eerste indrukken: Memoires van een driejarige (First Impressions: Memoirs of a Three-Year-Old). Querido, 1979. Novel.
Beweegredenen (Motives). Querido, 1982. Novel.

Translations:
In *Dremples* (Amsterdam), 7/8 (1979), pp. 4–13.

PAUL SNOEK (1933–1981)

Poetry:
Verzamelde gedichten (Collected Poems). Antwerp: Manteau, 1982. [All poems]

Other Works:
Reptielen & amfibieën (Reptiles & Amphibians). Bezige Bij, 1957. Stories.
With Hugues C. Pernath, *Soldatenbrieven* (Soldiers' Letters). Antwerp: Ontwikkeling / Bezige Bij, 1961.

Bultaco 250 cc. Brussels: Manteau, 1971. Stories.
Een hondsdolle tijd (A Mad-Dog Time). Brussels & The Hague: Manteau, 1978. Novel.

Translations:
With Martien Coppens (photographer), *Betwixt Land and Sea.* Translated by James S Holmes and Hans van Marle. Venlo, the Netherlands: no publisher listed [Van der Grinten], n.d. [c. 1964]. Poems and prose poems.
In the Sleep-Trap. Translated by Peter Nijmeijer. New Malden, England: Tangent Books, 1976.
In *Delta* (Amsterdam), Summer 1965, pp. 23, 40, 49–53, 62; Peter Nijmeijer (ed.), *Four Flemish Poets* (London: Transgravity Press, 1976), pp. 17–26; *Dremples* (Amsterdam), 3 (1976), pp. 26–40.

HANS TENTIJE (1944–   )

Poetry:
Alles is er (It's All There). Harmonie, 1975. ["Ikaries is de zee"]
Wat ze zei en andere gedichten (What She Said and Other Poems). Harmonie, 1978. ["Schepen, rivieren"]
Nachtwit (Night White). Harmonie, 1982.

Translations:
In *Contemporary Literature in Translation* (Vancouver), 32 (1981), pp. 17–20.

JOTIE T'HOOFT (1956–1977)

Poetry:
Verzamelde gedichten (Collected Poems). Antwerp: Manteau, 1982. [All poems]

Other Work:
Verzameld proza (Collected Prose). Antwerp: Manteau, 1982.

Translations:
In *Dremples* (Amsterdam), 7/8 (1979), pp. 97–106.

HANS VERHAGEN (1939–   )

Poetry:
Rozen & motoren (Roses and Motorcycles). Bezige Bij, 1963. ["Hans Verhagen & Zn."]
Cocon (Cocoon). Thomas Rap, 1966.

Sterren cirkels bellen (Stars Circles Bells). Bezige Bij, 1968. ["Kanker / Cancer / Krebs," "Sterren"]
Duizenden zonsondergangen (Thousands of Sunsets). Bezige Bij, 1973.
Koude voeten (Cold Feet). Bezige Bij, 1983.

Translations:
Euthanasia. Translated by Peter Nijmeijer. London: Joe DiMaggio Press, 1972.
Cocoon. Translated by Peter Nijmeijer. London: Transgravity Press, 1973.
Stars over Bombay. Translated by Peter Nijmeijer. London: Transgravity Press, 1976. Selected poems.

HANS VLEK (1947–   )

Poetry:
Zwart op wit (Black on White). Querido, 1970. [All poems]
Voor de bakker (In Order). Querido, 1972.
De toren van Babbel (The Tower of Babble). Querido, 1979.
Onnette sonnetten (Unclean Sonnets). Peter van der Velden, 1980.
Geen volkse god in uw achtertuin (No Folkish God in Your Back Garden). Querido, 1980. Selected poems.

EDDY VAN VLIET (1942–   )

Poetry:
De vierschaar: Gedichten 1962–1972 (The Judgment Seat: Poems 1962–1972). Brussels: Manteau / Paris, 1973. ["Geboorte"]
Het grote verdriet (The Great Sadness). The Hague & Rotterdam: Nijgh & Van Ditmar, 1974. ["In deze uitputtende lage landen"]
Na de wetten van afscheid & herfst (After the Laws of Goodbye & Autumn). Bezige Bij, 1978. [Four poems from *Na de wetten van afscheid & herfst*, "De kustlijn verandert niet voor de vissen"]
Glazen (Glasses). Bezige Bij, 1979. ["Oud champagneglas"]
Jaren na maart (Years after March). Bezige Bij, 1983. ["Groen. Ik herschrijf"]
[Uncollected: "Stockholm"]

Translations:
In *Delta* (Amsterdam), Autumn 1973, pp. 25–30; Konrad Hopkins and Ronald van Roekel (eds.), *Quartet* (Paisley, Scotland: Wilfion Books, 1978), pp. 44–57; *Contemporary Literature in Translation* (Vancouver), 32 (1981), pp. 46–49.

LEO VROMAN (1915–   )

Poetry:
262 gedichten (262 Poems). Querido, 1974. [All poems]
Huis en tuin (House and Garden). Querido, 1979.
Nieuwsgierig (Curious). Querido, 1980.
Het verdoemd carillon (The Doomed Carillon). Querido, 1981.
Liefde, sterk vergroot (Love, Highly Magnified). Querido, 1981.
Avondgymnastiek (Evening Gymnastics). Querido, 1983.

Other Works:
Tineke / De adem van Mars / Snippers (Tineke / The Breath of Mars / Snippets). Querido, 1960. Reprinted as *Proza* (Prose), Querido, 1966. Novellas.
Het Grauwse Diep (The Deep at Grauw). Querido, 1966. Drama.
Voorgrond, achtergrond (Foreground, Background). Querido, 1969. Drama.
Het carnarium (The Carnarium). Querido, 1973. Prose texts.
Brieven uit Brooklyn (Letters from Brooklyn). Querido, 1979. Letters.

Translations and Writings in English:
Poems in English. Querido, 1953. These and other poems in English are included in *262 gedichten* (see above).
Just One More World. Querido, 1976.
In *Delta* (Amsterdam), Spring/Summer 1966, pp. 64–66, 95–97, 117, 125.
Blood. Garden City, New York: Natural History Press, 1967. Study.

HANS WARREN (1921–   )

Poetry:
Verzamelde gedichten 1941–1981 (Collected Poems 1941–1981). Bert Bakker, 1982. [All poems]
Dit is werkelijk voor jou geschreven: Een bloemlezing uit eigen werk (This Really Was Written for You: An Anthology from His Own Work). Bert Bakker, 1982. Selected poems.

Other Works:
Nachtvogels (Night Birds). Arnhem: S. Gouda Quint & D. Brouwer, 1949. Study.
Kritieken (Criticism). Middelburg, the Netherlands: Provinciale Zeeuwse Courant, 1970. Essays.
Geheim dagboek (Secret Diary). Bert Bakker, 1981, 1982, 1983. Diary. Three volumes to date.

RIEKUS WASKOWSKY (1932–1977)

Poetry:
Tant pis pour le clown (A Pity for the Clown). Bezige Bij, 1966. ["Salt Peanuts," "Essay"]
Slechts de namen der grote drinkers leven voort (Only the Names of the Great Drinkers Endure). Bezige Bij, 1968. ["Wenn man unter Ewigkeit," "Dass die Sonne morgen aufgehen wird"]
Wie het eerst zijn steen kwijt is (He Who First Gets Rid of His Stone). Bezige Bij, 1970.

AD ZUIDERENT (1944–   )

Poetry:
Met de apocalyptische mocassins van Michel de Nostradame op reis door Nederland (Traveling through the Netherlands in Nostradamus' Apocalyptic Mocassins). Arbeiderspers, 1968.
De afstand tot de aarde (The Distance to the Earth). Arbeiderspers, 1974.
Geheugen voor landschap (Memory for Landscape). Arbeiderspers, 1979. ["Naar de eenzaamheid," "Huis aan de rivier," "Tot de verbeelding sprekend"]
[Uncollected: "Gebaar van verstandhouding"]

Translations:
Cycling, Recycling. Arbeiderspers, 1984. Selected poems translated into various languages.
In *Dremples* (Amsterdam), 7/8 (1979), pp. 44–53.

BOOKS IN ENGLISH BY OTHER CONTEMPORARY DUTCH-LANGUAGE POETS

Harry Brander, *What Rhymes with Cancer?* Translated by Judy Schavrien. Saint Paul: New Rivers Press, 1982.
Gaston Burssens, *From the Flemish of Gaston Burssens.* Translated by John Stevens Wade. Newton, Maine: Arts End Books, 1982.
Harry Hoogstraten, *Boxing Days: Poems & Visuals 1975–1979.* Haarlem: In de Knipscheer, 1979. Written in English.
Ed. Hoornik, *The Fish: A Long Poem.* Translated by Koos Schuur. Delta, 1965.
Harry Mulisch, *What Poetry Is.* Translated by Claire Nicolas White. Merrick, New York: Cross-Cultural Communications, 1982.
Willem M. Roggeman, *The Revolution Begins in Bruges.* Translated by Dorothy Howard and Hendrika Ruger. Windsor, Ontario: Netherlandic Press, 1983.

Index of Poets

Index of Translators